THE POWER OF POSITIVE PURPOSE

SECOND EDITION

THE POWER OF POSITIVE PURPOSE

JAY SCOTT NEALE

MEDIA

Published 2024 by Gildan Media LLC
aka G&D Media
www.GandDmedia.com

Front cover design by David Rheinhardt of Pyrographx

Designed by Meghan Day Healey of Story Horse, LLC.

Library of Congress Cataloging-in-Publication Data is available upon request

ISBN: 978-1-7225-0671-1

10 9 8 7 6 5 4 3 2 1

To the loving memory of Dr. Carol Ann Neale, who touched the lives of thousands of New Thought students with her intelligence, love, courage, and metaphysical understanding. As my wife, copastor, and mother of our children, she gave me a life of love, joy, and never-ending support. Carol taught me how to be teachable. She will always be in our hearts.

To my children (Jay, Paul, Lisa, Lynn, and Leslie) and my grandchildren (Eric, Tara, Taylor, and Trevor) and to my great-grandchildren: you give my life meaning I would not have without you. I love you.

To my teachers: Dr. William H. D. Hornaday, Dr. Craig Carter, Dr. Reginald C. Armor, Dr. Edith Clark, and Dr. Fenwicke Holmes. And to Cynthia C. C. Cavalcanti, who made this dream a reality.

Contents

Foreword

By Paula Langguth Ryan

"Dr. Jay" was not a humble man by any means. And that's a good thing. He exuded the power of presence. And he embodied the power of a positive purpose. But it wasn't always that way.

In the 1960s, he was a struggling actor in Los Angeles who used the teachings of Religious Science (also known as Science of Mind) to deal with the death of five friends killed in Vietnam as well as his own issues about his alcoholic father.

Jay and I became acquainted in 2014 while I was visiting the conference bookstore at that year's International New Thought Alliance Congress. Looking for gems not already on my shelves, I compiled a grouping and asked him off-handedly which four titles he'd most recommend. I barely remember three of the titles he selected from my pile. The fourth, he proudly proclaimed, was the best in the bunch. It was his book, *The Power of a Positive Purpose*.

Now I've read hundreds (maybe even thousands) of New Thought and self-help books. And I can honestly say this is the best book I've ever read. It's the most concise and complete guide to the inner work needed to harness the power of dynamic affirmative prayer and boldly transform our lives.

For six months, I read this book repeatedly. My copy is dog-eared, heavily underlined, filled with notes; I even cracked the spine and have to keep stuffing the pages back in.

How could I have missed this book when it was released in 2007? For starters, he'd self-published with zero contact information, no ISBN, nothing.

Long story short, I convinced Jay to allow me to reorganize the book and reissue it in a new second edition. It was originally a series of eighty-seven essays he'd written during a span of over twenty years. Now it's a seamless journey to transforming anything you think stands in your way.

Thoroughly grounded in spiritual truth. Boisterously born of true confidence—his and our own. From a mind that was directed by unlimited good. From a man who lived a life of love unfolding. Jay made his transition in April 2022, while we were still in the process of bringing forth the book you're reading.

Here's how I encourage you to read this book. First, hold a particular concern or pressing issue in mind. Then start reading. Apply the principles of these pages to the situation in your mind. Give that situation to "transformation" and consciously note (heck, even write down) the shifts you experience, the softening, the expansion, the uplifting.

After you feel one issue has been resolved within you, bring the next situation or attribute or thought to mind and do it again. And again. With a seemingly effortless ease, you will find that your grievances, fears, anger, doubts are all dissolved as you embrace and begin living from the power of a positive purpose.

Take these actions, and like Dr. Jay, you will find you're living a life that's a celebration of love. I can't think of a better inheritance for him to have left us.

Introduction

By Jay Scott Neale

The aim of this book is to inspire you to move in consciousness from thinking *about* purpose to thinking *from* purpose and as such to celebrate living more effectively.

The mystics of every age and location have all agreed with one another about what is true and why they let this Truth be their way. The path is learning to see as Truth sees; it is thinking about Truth as Truth thinks.

The directive to let the Mind be in you that was also in the great, the good, and the wise is this: do not just *think* about those who lived with great purpose; *learn* how to think as they thought and understand *why* they thought as they thought.

All great teachers have taught us that we can do this. We can spiritualize our intellect. This moves our consciousness in the right direction.

Central to the Science of Mind teaching is the idea that *there is nothing to heal*. Rather, there is a choice within each of us waiting to outperform all other choices. The Universe does not know what is going to happen to us until we make up our mind. As Ralph Waldo Emerson wisely stated, "We are what we think about all day long."

If you have set a goal for your life, ask yourself, "What is my purpose for achieving this goal?"

Then *become* the purpose of your goal—in action. Think as your purpose thinks, give as it gives, receive as it receives, and you will achieve your goal and more.

Raymond Charles Barker, a leader in the Religious Science movement, would wake his students up by having them Affirm: "I am the Voice of God, explaining Itself to Itself, by means of me."

The greatest teachers have all taught that what we are looking *for* is what we are looking *with*. Truth is not Truth unless it leads you to yourself. If it is leading you somewhere else, it is suspect.

As you flow through each part of *The Power of Positive Purpose*, you will strengthen these six attributes:

1. **Awareness.** The Kingdom of Infinite Life is within everyone, but not everyone is conscious of it.

2. **Adventure.** Once we wake up and become aware of spiritual Truth, life becomes an adventure in watching the miracle of Mind in action.

3. **Fun.** Learning the art of getting more enjoyment out of life is essential.

4. **Sticktoitiveness.** Too many people quit within a few steps of success. By staying the course, you'll break that cycle for yourself.

5. **Expectancy.** As you maintain a quality of expectation for your positive purpose, results will take care of themselves—and then some.

6 **Thankfulness.** Making the best possible use of gratitude for what we already have makes room for better things. To paraphrase Robert Browning, our reach must be higher than our grasp, or what's heaven for?

Our awareness as the Awakened Mind in action allows us to free ourselves into the *now*. We must know, without doubt, that we are greater, wiser, more intelligent, powerful, and loving than we ever let ourselves think we are. Now comes the courage to be what we think we know. This is letting go and being awakened inspiration in action. This is the Power of Positive Purpose.

Chapter One

The Power of Infinite Mind

The power of Infinite Mind is the power within us that creates. We each have the ability to develop this higher state of consciousness, which is always within us. The great teachers have all affirmed that we each deserve the fulfilled, perfect development of the Spirit in us *as us*, which is the nature of God, the only Creator.

How long does it take to accomplish this? Forever! But as we move in consciousness from where we are to where we can be, we begin to realize that each day in every way, the best keeps getting better all the time.

Letting go and letting the reality of Divine Principle sink in and become our way begins when we understand God to be the Creator of all. It is That Which Creates.

Looking into the matter seriously, we find that Intelligent Spirit creates all things by means of us. This is what the great have defined as God or Spirit. When we pay attention to it *as* us, we receive its invitation to accept its way, truth, and life as our experience, our reason and purpose for being here.

Our challenge is to conceive of ourselves as individualizations of Infinite Intelligence, of Spirit, just as a drop of the ocean is an individualized entity within the ocean. The reality of Principle enables us to believe that we are individualizations of the same and only Creative Spirit of Infinite Life.

We start our discovery of this truth by asking ourselves these six questions:

1. Do I still prefer to know myself as an individualization of the world?
2. Am I still judging from the standpoint of the world?
3. Am I choosing to surrender my divine birthright?
4. Do I need to awaken to a greater idea of myself?
5. Do I honor the teachings of the great, the good, and the wise of every age and accept the Light that lights every person?
6. Is my present reality happy, healthy, abundant, loving, and loved?

As we develop the reality of Principle and the consciousness of its power in us, as us, we discover we are truly perfecting our way, demonstrating success and giving to our world in an inspirationally positive way. As we gain greater and greater understanding of Truth, we find ourselves free from false beliefs in limitation, doubt, and fear.

Affirm: *God's Way, Truth, and Life are my experience, my reason, and my purpose for being here.*

There is no limit to Spirit except the limit we ourselves put upon it. The development of the reality of Principle permits us to flow through our life experience victoriously.

We are unparalleled good in action, blessing every life we touch. We have been told, "Seek and ye shall find." Find what? The Way, which is ready, willing, and able to demonstrate itself for the benefit of all people, everywhere.

Form Immovable Faith

Many people consider Mahatma Gandhi's famous 1931 speech, delivered at Kingsley Hall, London, to be his statement of faith. As part of that speech, he shared these wise words:

> I do dimly perceive that whilst everything around me is ever changing, ever dying, there is underlying all that change a living Power that is changeless, that holds all together, that creates, dissolves and recreates. That informing Power of Spirit is God. . . . This realization is preceded by an immovable faith.

As students of metaphysics, we discover how thoughts and attitudes affect our relationships, pocketbooks, circumstances, and health. Mind, thought, and the world are one and the same thing. Our material reality is "thick thought." Everything is everything else because the realm of the Power of Spirit is everywhere at once.

As we discover and yield to our higher spiritual awareness and true Self, we understand more and more that nothing is separate from Divine Mind. We know every day is filled with

opportunities for seeking and discovering a greater understanding of truth, independent of dogma, creed, or ceremony,
and free from superstition.

There is one Mind—the Mind of God—and all experience
and all beings are in and of this Mind. The great, the good, and
the wise of every age have examined and grasped this idea.

Spiritual Mind Treatment, or affirmative prayer, is the
movement from awareness of the One Mind to conscious
unity with it, to realization and grateful acceptance of the
material event with immovable faith. It is God flowing from
itself, through itself, to itself, by means of you and me.

The mystic minds of every age tell us over and over again
that Infinite Mind is the primary source of existence of everything that has been, is now, and will be, and that all is happening at once. It is the formless, intangible, forever becoming
tangible by way of our belief. When we know this and know
that we know it, we experience our own souls greeting themselves as our lives and everyone in them.

In Galileo's time, people had difficulty believing the
earth revolved around the sun. The master teacher Jesus
taught, "It is done unto you as you believe," and for more
than 2,000 years, people have had difficulty believing that
lesson as well.

Eight years after Gandhi delivered his statement of faith,
Ernest Holmes, the founder of Religious Science, penned *The
Science of Mind*, in which he wrote, "Love is Self-givingness
through creation, the impartation of the Divine through the
human." Our challenge now is to wake up and realize that
transforming our world by the renewing of our minds is not
difficult. What can be difficult is choosing to do it.

Immovable faith is the key to the treasure chest of whole-ness, creativity, and love. Well-being in all our relationships, the deep joy of self-awareness, and the capacity to live as a positive part of the whole *are all ours to choose*. Only one thing stands between us and our choices.

Conform or Transform

The wisest and clearest minds of the ages have taught us we must warmly express love if we are to feel love. The love of others and its return to us is an aspect of God rejoicing in Itself.

This is the universal Law of Attraction, which is set in motion by way of our thought. This experience is also called positive prayer, or Spiritual Mind Treatment. Treatment is *not* something we do to make things happen; it is something we do to describe what has already happened in Truth. As we know it, feel it, affirm it, and embody it, we automati-cally rejoice in harmonious, full, and rich encounters and relationships.

We love enough to give our very best. Because we move from within ourselves—carrying in thought, word and deed, the love of our intelligence, talent, creativity, health, happi-ness, and success—the length and breadth of our environ-ment is decorated by way of our thinking.

Spiritual Mind Treatment is synonymous with positive faith, evolving as healthy mind, body, and world, which is our natural state of being. Psalm 144:9 exemplifies this positive faith with praise to God: every day "I will sing a new song unto thee."

Positive faith forever sings a new song because it is creativity and happiness. I use the term *positive faith* because we can always choose the experience of faith in the negative, expressed as worry, doubt, and fear. Negative states are only the results of faith that everything is going to go wrong. Positive or negative, our use of faith is always our choice.

We must always make sure not to confuse faith with *fate*. Both acknowledge a power in and through life, but faith is the intelligent self-direction we experience when we discover within us the Providence that will do anything if we let go and let It act.

With God, all things are possible. We become aware we are sharing views, objectives, and inspiration with all the great, the good and the wise. We discover new and wonderful ways and means for accomplishing our goals and dreams. Faith in the positive sets in motion the Power that answers prayers.

Positive faith loves daily work, rest, and play, while belief in fate creates an experience of life that is passive and negative. It is void of the exhilarating intimacy of faith in the positive. Fate grovels before a predicament. Positive faith, centered in love, goes boldly forth to meet a predicament before it raises its ugly head.

Fate deteriorates with time. Positive faith becomes bolder lovingly as it grows older beautifully. As it has been written, "the Lord is my shepherd; I shall not want" (Psalm 23:1).

Romans 12:2 tells us to be not conformed to this world, but to be transformed by the renewing of our mind. This tells us clearly that we should not allow our minds to be filled with fear, condemnation, or a belief in limitation, which is the thought pattern dominant in the world today. This kind of thinking produces sickness, poverty, loneliness, and heartache.

Spiritual Mind Treatment transforms our lives by establishing a new thought pattern built on the Infinite Principle within, the love of Truth, and an understanding of our unity with God and everyone everywhere. Spiritual Mind Treatment gives the Creative Power an opportunity to express Its own nature. Health and harmony become visible as effortlessly as the sun rises each morning.

When our distorted thinking is removed, our distorted world is healed. Spiritual Mind Treatment removes distorted thinking. Our minds are renewed by taking this idea as the basis of our thinking: *since God is all there is, all that is, is God.*

In her book *In His Name,* spiritual practitioner and author Lillian DeWaters wrote:

It makes no difference to Truth whether you view it as Truth or as evil. Truth is Truth nevertheless and is all there is, and even while you feel sick, or lame, or sinful, still, at that very instant, you are only one way — you are perfect immortal being, and what you call sickness and sinfulness never touch real being. Can you grasp this deep fact of Life? This is the vision that rends the veil. This is the vision that causes one to leap from his bed and refuse any longer to be in prison, for what prison can hold a spirited being!

Bound by Belief

Raymond Charles Barker continually emphasized that it is never our *appearances* but only our *belief* that binds us. This was the foundation of his ministry and is the heart of Science of Mind teaching.

What we demonstrate as experience cannot go beyond our belief about ourselves. The spiritually bored have not yet awakened to this understanding; hence they often look outside to various teachings and teachers. But powerful teachings and true teachers lead us to *ourselves*. Spiritual health is knowing we are each the message and the messenger. Truth is not Truth unless it leads us to our inner Self.

Money, people, places, and things are never the problem or the answer; consciousness is. A good question to ask ourselves is, "Am I meeting expectations or just setting them?" All our dreams are waiting for us to come true. Unless we commit to that which is above our current consciousness, we will yield to that which is around us. What plan would we have on our drawing board of life if we had all the support we need to fulfill those plans?

Plan your work, and work your plan. Success is two four-letter words: *plan* and *work*. Sell yourself on your dreams and your vision; think as they think, see as they see, and stick with it!

This is spiritual self-leadership in action and high spiritual self-esteem unfolding. We discover our unlimited potential as a sense of accomplishment and pride in what we are and what we do. This is a great science, but it has to be understood—and we are the ones who must understand it. We are the mighty, moving Power of Intelligent Love.

When we have the consciousness of love, success, and happiness, nothing can stop it from filling our experience.

Consciousness cannot be taught; it must be imparted. No matter where you are or what you are doing, know that this higher consciousness is there—that God is there.

Affirm: *I am the Voice of Infinite Mind, explaining Itself to Itself by means of me.*

Ralph Waldo Emerson shared the powerful idea that we are what we think about all day long. Think about what you think about. Remember Barker's creed: "Only our belief, and never appearances, binds us." And let the wonderful be your way.

Harness Maximum-Strength Metaphysics

The only thing a scrambled mind has to look forward to is a question mark. The only thing a clear mind has to look forward to is the best getting better.

This is the power of using the One Principle within us all. If we have a problem in life, we can release the choice of doubt, despair, and the consciousness, which caused the problem, and put the matter in its proper place. Through positive choosing and being, we achieve wonderful, lifelong development and growth.

No one can be a success in the art of living by pretending to be something other than what he or she is. What are we? A mighty, moving power of Divine Mind in action.

Affirm: *I am a mighty, moving power of Divine Mind in action.*

We are the God-created expression of beingness forever seeking to increase Its fulfillment. Our thinking is the trigger for activating our experience; therefore, it never pays to ignore the future we are creating in this very moment.

If anyone is just floating complacently, accepting a limited experience in happiness, health, or wealth, she can take the reins of positive self-direction and become maximum-strength metaphysics in action. The German philosopher G. W. F. Hegel wrote about his belief that evolution is the never-ending flow of Divine Consciousness out of itself: all creation, continually moving, never arrives at any state other than that of a ceaseless flow.

Infinite Greatness always expresses itself through positive self-awareness, made manifest in the consciousness of the individual. Positive self-awareness is the cause of a perfect, harmonious, and beautiful life. It heals the darkness and confusions of life.

To change our lives for the better, we must change our minds for the better and choose to make it permanent. Ernest Holmes believed that the key to the healing process was to change your mind and keep it changed.

With persistent practice and definite purpose, we can let go and let maximum-strength metaphysics assert itself as our way. When we exercise positive patience and vigilance, our daily great reward cannot be denied.

We are one with the perfect power, health, and life of Infinite Intelligence. As we become more aware of this Truth—in and as our experience—we discover it is easy to make it permanent in our life. We do this by turning away from doubt or fear and walking in the light, by informing our minds of the unlimited Truth of our Being.

Affirm: *I am one with the perfect power, health, and life of Infinite Intelligence.*

This is our divine birthright. As we insistently and eagerly claim it, we unfold as fulfillment everywhere at once.

Establish the Attitude of High Expectancy

All belief has a way of becoming our experiences—desirable or undesirable. Our belief gives birth to the choices we make.

The *way* is the Law of Infinite Mind, in us, as us. The *experience* is the result or effect of our belief in action. In reality, our world is nothing more than "thick thought."

Does what you define as "greater good" seem to be lacking in your experience? Is your reaction time—moving in consciousness from problem to solution—slower than you know it can be? Does achieving a successful level of positive demonstration seem like a fading dream?

Removing ourselves from the horns of a dilemma arising from thick thinking requires a healthy commitment of positive self-direction. The poet e. e. cummings summed this up perfectly by saying, in essence, that a person who does not look for a forever new cause will always live with a forever old effect.

Positive self-direction becomes our way when we let what we really want to change or accomplish be the advancing front edge of our consciousness—uncontaminated by negative or fearful thinking. We are a direct idea in the Mind of the Infinite. It has direct knowledge *of* us because it *is* us. As we let this Truth be the essence of our choices, we find we can make choices with the strength of spiritual insight, and we discover ourselves celebrating our outstanding experience.

Our daily responsibility to ourselves is to relax in our awareness that the Universe is friendly. All the infinite creativity of the Universe is always available and ready to fulfill itself as our health, happiness, and success.

Affirm: *The Health of Divine Mind is my healthy experience. The Intelligence of Divine Mind is my living teacher. The Light of Divine Mind is my steadfast guide.*

It is easy to understand a child who is afraid of the dark. What is truly sad is an adult who is afraid of the light. To live in the Light of Divine Mind, free from fear, is to open our mind to positive demonstration beyond the scope of our routine thinking. We then honor Spirit as our healthy experience, learn from it as our living teacher, and allow its direction to be our direction. With the Light of Infinite Wisdom, we can fully understand our oneness with positive self-expression and growth.

Our conviction about our highest desires keeps them alive as our health and freedom. We can seek and find that which we require from life, and better, in the attitude of high expectancy.

Discover God's Perfection

The question, "What is God?" has been asked since humankind was first able to formulate questions. In order to understand God—Infinite Life—and our relationship with it, we must learn how to know ourselves as Divine Life.

According to the teachings of the Indian sage Sri Ramakrishna, those who don't find the Eternal in themselves will never find it outside, but those who see the Eternal in the temple of their own soul will see the Eternal also in the temple of the Universe.

The greatest thinkers of every age teach us that God is good, and the good is God. We are also told God is Love and that in Love there is no condemnation. Love forgives everything. Love is the fulfilling of the law of our being.

If we come into a true consciousness or inner state of love, we have at that moment become the consciousness of God in us, as us. This is the experience of Christ consciousness.

When we are aware of our good, we can no longer be aware of less than good. Our good consists of what we need right now to take the next step on the wonderful road of life and be more than we have ever been before.

The Divine Plan is that all our needs are met and that greater good is at our disposal now. The Bhagavad Gita teaches that those who see rightly are those who behold the Supreme Lord dwelling equally in all existence eternally.

Poets are aligned with this idea as well. In his poem "Saul," Robert Browning wrote:

> *I but open my eyes,—and perfection, no more and no less,*
> *In the kind I imagined, full-fronts me, and God is seen God*
> *In the star, in the stone, in the flesh, in the soul and the clod.*

Elizabeth Barrett Browning impressed the thinking world with similar observation in her epic poem "Aurora Leigh":

Earth's crammed with Heaven
And every common bush afire with God;
But only he who sees takes off his shoes.

Lifting our consciousness from the narrow confines of human thinking, acting, and reacting, we claim our innate ability to see beyond the obvious. We can celebrate the truth of our existence and the actuality of everything, everywhere at once. Author Harriet Beecher Stowe believed that in all ranks of life, the human heart yearns for the beautiful, and the beautiful things that God makes are a Divine gift to all.

The truth of Divine Mind may be hidden from us as fog hides the beauty of the world around us, but the beauty and potential of the world are always there. Health, prosperity, and love are always there for us to see if we choose to dispel the fog of doubt, fear, and confusion.

God *in* the perfection of form, *as* the perfection of form, *is* the perfection of form. We are each the reflection of its greatness. Our challenge is to let that which is divinely inherent within us see the truth now. Our divine heritage is our capacity to appreciate and recreate the goodness and harmony of God as the sum of our lives.

Affirm: *Divine Life in me, as me, is me. All that is divinely inherent within me sees this Truth and acts from it, now.*

Chapter Two

Infinite Power Creates Greater Things

The grand thinkers of every age have told us that the Truth and Principle of Infinite Intelligence are the Truth and Principle of our being. When we know this, and know we know it, we can live our lives and love what we are choosing to do with them. Our daily affirmation becomes, "I am here. It is now. I am alive, and I matter."

Intelligence, teachability, and positive experimentation in the face of everyday experience are invitations to unlimited success. Each of us is the unlimited Power of Positive Principle in action. As we direct our lives from this awareness, we rid ourselves of risk and let affirmative certainty be our way. Happiness, unequivocal power, and confident commitment are required in the presence of Life, heaven-bent on our healthy unfoldment.

In living and loving from Principle, one rule applies: "Do unto others as you would have others do unto you." Following this rule, we are subject to "attacks" of greatness, and unexpected good fills our life from unexpected people, places, and things—from anyone and anything, anywhere. We are able to celebrate even the slightest opportunity to gain the upper hand in this wonderful thing called life.

When we become one with the reality of Principle, we free ourselves of "stinking thinking" and see that greater health, abundance, happiness, and good are lovingly unavoidable. Our positive responsiveness makes the entire situation better and better. Stinking thinking never changed anyone's life for the better, but confident thinking and endeavor will demonstrate the wonderful—everywhere at once.

Confident thinking requires mastery of the Truth of Self. As author and philosopher Elbert Hubbard wrote, men do not accomplish greater things because they do not undertake greater things.

When the reality of Principle is our way, we undertake greater things and discover we are fanning a spark of positive desire (the Divine Urge) into a brightly burning flame within our hearts. This kind of self-discovery guarantees success and the greatest adventure of all, because we are choosing to work in harmony with the great spiritual Principle of the Universe. Our life becomes a feast of marvels, our demonstrations become dazzling, and we discover we understand the Infinite as never before.

At the core of human experience are the heart and mind; at the core of both heart and mind is Principle. The search for Infinite Intelligence in a Divine Universe leads to the awareness that, as Ernest Holmes stated, "What we are searching for, we are searching with." We become tireless proponents of our positive spiritual heritage.

Affirm: *I am here. It is now. I am alive, and I matter.*

Practice the Way of Nonresistance

When we choose a defensive or obstructing action in our thoughts, we set up detrimental causation. It makes no essential difference whether the resistance seems justifiable or not; the result is the same. It abuses us as well as others. This is why the master teacher Jesus told us to do good to them that hate and turn the other cheek in order to reveal the perfection of our heavenly Creator.

In Matthew 5:39, we're told, "Resist not evil." Nonresistance as the foundation of our relationship to the world is the way of God in us, as us. It is the way of God, greeting itself as our existence.

As we learn to live in perfect alignment with Divine Love, no action of resistance can touch us. We accomplish this alignment by taking these five steps:

1. **Realize that problems cannot survive the presence of Reality.** As we do, we embody the very essence and principles of intelligence, love, health, happiness, and success. We are free. We are all children of God.

Affirm: *I stop thinking about what I am and let what I am do the thinking. I am nonresistance in action right now!*

2. **Live for the moment rather than living in the moment.** Our daily commitment is to get out of our own heads and into our Being. As we do, we no longer waste time trying to make ourselves all right by making everyone else all right (or all wrong!). Within each of us is a creative urge that is a vital part of Life itself. Our personal mission statement becomes, *All is right with my world. I now create and live!*

3. **Live as if greatness is a necessity.** Our understanding of Truth will serve us well. If it is not serving us, we need to understand that there is simply more to understand. The time for upgrading consciousness is always *now*. We must never rest in our commitment to the Truth of our being. The eternal Creative Spirit within us desires us to fulfill our part in the greatness of All That Is.

4. **Hear the bell before it rings.** In *Winds of Hiroshima*, the American philosopher Ralph Tyler Flewelling wrote that "understanding and power lie in the relationship of our spirits to the Eternal Creative Spirit which is but another name for the Living God." We contact our ability to hear the bell before it rings by entering the secret place of the Most High in our consciousness (see Psalm 91:1). We let go of every concept of lack or failure. We let go of any traits of personality and temperament that have given birth to less than the best in us. As we contemplate a greater expression of life than we have ever before accepted, God's Spirit supplies us with new and perfect ideas. We hear the bell before it rings and see beyond any appearance. We welcome our new awareness and use it in gratitude and joy.

Affirm: *I now learn how to disengage from any stress, and all causes of it.*

5. **Know that perception fuels consciousness.** When we wake up and realize we no longer live in the consciousness of the inadequacies of our past, our perceptions of the present moment change for the better, and our future improves. We know our successes do not depend on circumstance, place, or person, but on the caliber of our own thought, devotion, and commitment to our chosen activities. Psalm 37:5 tells us to commit our way to the Lord, trust Him, and He shall "bring it to pass." This nonresistant way of taking charge of our living unfolds as we know (and know that we know) that the unfailing Law of Mind acts upon our acceptance, bringing forth a perfect result in a perfect way. It is a wonderful thing to let go and allow our thinking to be in accord with God's perfection.

When we decide that the substance of our experience shall more and more reflect the glory of God's Life *as* us, we find fulfillment of every desire. God's wisdom, bounty, peace, and love happen in a step by step, moment by moment advance in consciousness.

Nonresistance is the power at the heart of God. Nothing can attack or resist it. If we let this revelation become a vital way of living, we can affirm that the way of our heart is the heart of our way—and know what we are talking about.

Trying to pressure others into changing their lives for the better is a major cause of unhappiness. If you want someone to change for the better, realize it is hopeless except by way of example—being to others as you would have them be to you.

Move from working on people to changing your own con-sciousness. This is easy when you do unto yourself as you would have others do unto you. Ask yourself, *what is the most loving thing I can do for myself in this moment?*

Direct your reactions to others in a positive way. Free them through your own awareness that Infinite Wisdom is moving them into greater expression. Remember that only those who have practiced this approach to interpersonal relationships can realize its benefits. When you choose to be in the loving action of your true and wonderful self, any division, conflict, or despair disappears.

Affirm: *Infinite Wisdom is moving me into greater expression.*

Apply Full-Vision Thinking

When excellence becomes tradition, there is no end to great-ness. What gets in the way of excellence becoming tradition? Lack of vision into the deeper meaning of things. Limited vision has two culprits. The first is ignorance. Ignorance is subject to a healing change of consciousness, and it is forgivable.

The second culprit is the closed mind. A mind closed to change and clearer understanding, meaning, and deeper truths is weak, foolish, and vulnerable. That is not the mind of a full-vision thinker; it is the mind of a boor.

In *Representative Men*, Emerson stated, "Belief consists in accepting the affirmations of the soul; unbelief, in denying them." What separates the full-vision thinker from the boor is the pursuit of philosophic understanding: the need to know that things are not merely as they seem, but vastly more simple and beautiful.

A full-vision thinker knows that if all we see is what we saw before, we are going to miss half of what is going on. The German philosopher Arthur Schopenhauer shared his deep understanding of this truth when he stated: "It is only after a man has got rid of all pretension, and taken refuge in mere unembellished existence, that he is able to attain that peace of mind which is the foundation of human happiness."

Our embodiment of this wisdom prevents us from being a song unsung. Otherwise, we will realize, as Indian poet Rabindranath Tagore wrote in his poem "Waiting," that

> *The song I came to sing*
> *remains unsung to this day.*
> *I have spent my days in stringing*
> *and in unstringing my instrument.*

We cannot expect the best of ourselves if we think aimlessly about our qualities. Determine, decide, and declare that you will not be a song unsung. Select a positive future to which you choose to pay special attention. Unless we do this, we will dissipate our energies and patience by living in compulsive, undirected activity.

Affirm: *I will not be a song unsung. I pay special attention to the positive future I have selected and joyously celebrate as it now unfolds.*

Full-vision thinkers consciously let go of all seemingly negative conditions. It does not matter what they may have endured; the negative is no longer part of their experience.

The moment we decide to get our limited idea of self out of the way and become full-vision thinkers, we achieve a sense of greatness that comes with the certain awareness of the unlimited Power that is always right where we are.

In Isaiah 58:8 we read, "Then shall thy light break forth as the morning, and thy health shall spring forth speedily." It is the pleasure of the Infinite Life that created us out of itself to give us the kingdom of our inherent magnificence. It is our responsibility to embody this kingdom fully and completely.

As we stop listening to the negative diagnoses of the people and events in our lives, we never again contemplate or expect less than the best. We get up every morning and say to ourselves, *"Remember, you have great things to do today!"* and then we do them.

Choose to be a full-vision thinker. As you choose, so you will be.

Affirm: *I have great things to do today! And I do them with a tradition of excellence.*

Reach the Zenith of Spiritual Awareness

With our vision expanded, we move in consciousness from *knowing* about our inner freedom to *discovering* how to think and act from it.

Every person has the power and right to think as freedom thinks. Too many people fail to claim this birthright and hence fail to do something wonderful with it. The great mind of Johann Wolfgang von Goethe gave us this insight from his renowned tragedy *Faust*:

> *Yes! to this thought I hold with firm persistence;*
> *The last results of wisdom stamps it true;*
> *He only earns his freedom and existence,*
> *Who daily conquers them anew.*

We attain the zenith of spiritual awareness when we reach the highest pinnacle of metaphysical consciousness and spring into a greater awareness of Divine Spirit. Metaphysically, this unfolds as the individual's recognition of his or her spiritual identity with Infinite Mind. This Infinite Mind never acts temperamentally or from external coercion, but in accordance with its own absoluteness. As Ernest Holmes taught, the thing we change is not Reality or the Law of Life or Mind, but our own action in it.

Consciously embracing these five mental actions aligns us with the One Mind:

1. Know it takes positive faith and practice to achieve positive success.
2. Reject negative thinking, and fill your heart and mind with the loving qualities of spiritual awareness.
3. Practice mindfulness, and open your thinking to new ideas.
4. Honor your inner desire to know and understand more.
5. Let love flow from the greatness of heart to the greatness of experience.

As the zenith of spiritual awareness in action, we can wisely nip limitation in the bud before it sets gloomily and heavily into our thinking. The clearest minds of the ages have passed down this lesson: life is beautiful, but the eye of the beholder must be free to see it so. We must be it in our awareness, to see it in our experience.

We are eternally seeking a greater form of expression. But if we are unwilling to feel appreciation for the fortune to be found in the present, greater blessings are unlikely to come our way. An ungrateful person rarely receives the fulfillment of his or her heart's desires. Furthermore, such a person stands an excellent chance of losing what he or she has already received. Our positive purpose thrives as we fill our hearts to overflowing with thanksgiving and praise.

Give thanks for your unity with God. For being alive in this wonderful world. For family friendship and warm, loving companionship. And for the gift of understanding and your ability to choose the positive. In this way, you will ensure the presence of good in your life.

All matter is simply Spirit compressed into form; the things of our world are Divine Substance with tangible use for us. Our Universe is based on a spiritual pattern of unlimited good, and no material manifestation of this Truth can in any way be less than the best.

As we honor the Divine Presence as the provider of all creation, which is made out of itself, we are free. When our thinking is balanced with this understanding, the necessities and comforts of life become the celebration of our way. We give the best, everywhere at once. We bless it, respect its proper value, and give thanks, knowing that what we send forth must return to us multiplied. Send forth the beautiful, centered in spiritual awareness.

Affirm: *My Universe is based on a spiritual pattern of unlimited good, and no material manifestation of this Truth can in any way be less than the best. I give the best of myself knowing, with gratitude, that the best flows to me in return.*

Exude Positive Faith

A law of reward does not exist in the Universe. The reward concept was created by human thinking in conforming to the world and causes most human hopelessness.

Sometimes people make statements such as:

I am good all the time, but God will not reward me.

I am loving, honest, and kind, but I am not a success.

I look at other people who are unloving and mean, and they are successful. I am good. Why does God reward them and punish me?

The law of the Universe is the law of cause unfolding as effect. A definite event or result evolves from a definite action or choice that is believed in and acted upon.

A person who commits himself to the positive and has faith in his success will prosper everywhere at once. Passive dependence on "just being good" to bring about financial or any other kind of success will more than likely fail. Active living and giving from the highest concept of good results in inner peace, positive self-esteem, a clear conscience, and a successful life at home, work, and play.

Positive faith, followed by action, is the one thing we can implement to let unlimited success be our commonplace experience. Students of metaphysics cannot be satisfied by, or content with, the idea of a limited God. If there were even one little thing it could not do, it would not be God and would not deserve our belief and faith.

We know Divine Mind is ever present and all-powerful, possessing infinite attributes that can never fail. If we establish in our own mind the awareness of the Allness of Infinite Intelligence—and our faith in it is complete in the action of good—we only have to let go and live by our positive convictions in regard to what it can and will do for us.

As we let this lesson be our way, we begin to astound our world and everyone in it. We know the happiest and most successful day of our lives is happening *now*. We even feel better physically.

Our body is made by the Spirit of Infinite Love, out of the Spirit of Infinite Love. Distorted physical manifestation cannot be a malfunction of Spirit, because the thought process of Divine Mind is always healthy.

You have been given the responsibility to be harmony in action. Harmony of consciousness reflects as harmony in your body and your world. When you substitute correct, healthy knowing for anything that is unlike it in your thinking, the result is the outpicturing of a healthy, perfectly functioning body and world.

Know that any negative idea or emotion that has temporarily manifested as a sensory testimony of illness is now erased. Center your thought on the harmony of Divine Spirit reflecting throughout your body, and be grateful that this healing is good enough to be true.

As our relationship with ourselves is improved, our relationships with others are more harmonious. Our work is accomplished with half the effort we previously put forth. We discover we are falling asleep at night with satisfaction and peace of mind. When we live in positive faith, we turn away from fear, indecision, and doubt, letting happiness, health, and security be our way.

Conform to Higher Aspirations

Everyone conforms to something, even if it is to nonconformity. Humans tend to form judgments about life and everything in it and then conform to that judgment.

People form judgments about what they are capable of being, doing, and demonstrating. Many times, they do not even contemplate a life beyond their past.

People who live, move, and have their being from the dualism of "world-mind thinking" fear the higher level clarity of the Mystic Mind, the part of us that is always thinking from Oneness. Worldly minded thinkers rebel at the discipline required to conform to this higher aspiration, which is above and beyond anything they have ever known.

In *The Creative Process in the Individual*, Thomas Troward wrote, "Relying on the maxim that Principle is not bound by Precedent we should not limit our expectations of the future. A principle dispossessed of restriction will heal, harmonize and prosper everything."

New opportunities present themselves to us when we remove limitations to God's right action *as* us. Answers take the place of problems, greater good appears unexpectedly, and the impossible becomes possible.

Confidence evolves as our power of choice, and we flow from where we are to where we can be with the joy of knowing that Principle is not bound by precedent. When a challenge appears and the world around us asks, "Why?" we ask, "Why not?" Why not conform to higher aspirations and go for it?

Embody Love in Action

The nineteenth-century British poet Philip James Bailey believed that everyone must think himself an act of God, that our mind is a thought of God, our life is a breath of God, and that we each should try—by great thoughts and good deeds—to show the most of the heaven we have within.

Every time a newborn child experiences its first breath, Infinite Life becomes a new and wonderful expression of itself. Divine Mind blesses each new form of itself with all that is needed for spiritual, mental, and physical progress and positive development. Every birth is the Christ Child coming forth into a new experience of itself.

Ernest Holmes likewise taught that the Infinite has already implanted within us an instinctive intuition, which is the spiritual knowledge of good, and that we evolve through an inner awakening to the powers, laws, and potentialities that already existed before we ever knew of them.

In Mark 11:25 it is written: "Forgive, if ye have aught against anyone, that your Father also who is in heaven may forgive you." The healing of mind, body, and world that happens in the lives of those who extend forgiveness is wonderful beyond words.

To get a clear understanding of the term *forgiveness*, we must forgive *and* forget. If we are unable to forget, we have not truly forgiven.

If we unwisely mull over things we need to forgive, we make ourselves receptive to their repetition. The sincerity of the forgiveness we offer to another measures the permanence and extent of the forgiveness we ourselves receive.

When we know this truth and unfold from it, we discover the glory of living with a positive purpose. We release limitation-producing thoughts of bitterness, jealousy, hurt feelings, irritation, or resentment. We do so without stress as we celebrate our self-esteem, self-confidence, and courage.

If we adopt this awareness, we must also learn to keep our living fully in the Presence of Infinite Love. We can learn to substitute active love for everything unlike it. We can rule out the negative and give birth to the affirmative when we let go and let God.

Affirm: *I now activate my Divine instinctive intuition and embrace the spiritual knowledge of good in my life. I let go and let Divine Love guide my thoughts and actions.*

Chapter Three

The Power of Self-Directed Consciousness

All too often, the image of our self that comes to mind is as a victim of circumstances or fate. This is an effect of a belief in a dual Universe. The power of self-directed consciousness begins with the awareness that, as e. e. cummings stated, "One's not half of two. It's two are halves of one." And in the *Gospel of Thomas*, Jesus tells us that when you make the two one, you will have discovered the kingdom of heaven. As we recognize this truth, we begin questioning our beliefs.

Questions we should all ask ourselves include: Is my concept of the Universe big enough? Is my concept of myself and the principle of the Power within me big enough?

The power of self-directed consciousness is the natural result of observing ourselves in a positive way, then observing ourselves observing ourselves. It is a celebration of the infinite Something in us, as us, that is uninterruptedly aware of every facet of our experience.

Once we recognize and acknowledge this truth, the next step is to nurture it. It will then serve as a medium for unlimited positive self-growth as we learn to move from thinking *about* it to the freedom of thinking *as* it.

As we achieve a belief in and an understanding of this highest concept of the age, our world converts itself into the wonderful arena it was meant to be, filled with unexpected good from unexpected people, places, and things. This follows the directive of Ephesians 4:23, which urges us to be renewed in the spirit of our mind.

As we identify with healthy-mindedness, we remove "disease" from our thought, body, and world. The power of creative, positive imagination becomes our advancing front edge, and any effects of past self-delusion are restored in the healthiest, happiest, and most harmonious way possible.

Within the panorama of Infinite Principle, there are no limitations of greatness. The challenge for us is to outshine our old way of being and assume a higher self-standard, with its new positive thought capability.

Jesus challenged us to end duality as a way of thinking and discover how to think from oneness when he stated that if our "eye be single," our whole body will be filled with light. We reach the point where our inner awareness and vision are concerned with the vitality of God's Presence indwelling us, when we become interested only in a totally whole and perfect state of being.

As such, our bodies reflect the luminescence of the celestial, which fills the Universe and unfolds as every created thing. When this vision is single and there are no dark shadows of belief in being apart from God, bodily perfection is experienced automatically.

By contemplation, we move into a consciousness of wholeness. Then our body, our world, and our experience mirror this understanding, which permanently heals and makes our lives beautiful.

To live, move, and have our being on the path of Divine Wisdom and Love becomes all-illuminating, all-expanding, all-uplifting, and all-embracing. Every healthy experience in life is an effect of the Divine Principle of Infinite Good unfolding from thought to thing.

In the consciousness of this wonderful life, we can practice positive right action. Just as many of the blessings we have today once seemed impossible, so too are the answers to our success now ready to demonstrate as our experience.

Affirm: *Something wonderful is happening now!*

Become a Wise Teacher

Letting the two become one as consciousness unfolds from the truth of itself is truly discovering the "kingdom" here and now.

People who let this wonderful awakening become their way reveal from within themselves a greatness that pulsates and promotes positive growth. They are fully aware of the inexhaustible perfection of vigor and energy that is the truth of everyone.

As we make the two into one in consciousness, we know that in order to change any situation for the better, we must give our spirit permission to command for the better. We are each eternal and free individuals, wonderful centers of intelligent self-manifestation in the Mind of God. This allows each of us to be a blessing to the material world of time and space through which we move; the material world then becomes a blessing to us.

> **Affirm:** *I am fully aware of the inexhaustible perfection and vigor that is my Truth and the Truth of all others.*

The Indian sage Sri Aurobindo wrote in *The Synthesis of Yoga* that the wise teacher will seek to *awaken* much more than to instruct. His work is a trust from above, he himself a channel, a vessel, a representative. He is a man helping his brothers, a child leading children, a light leading other lights, an awakened soul awakening other souls; at highest, a power or presence of the Divine calling to him other powers of the Divine.

When we awaken to the awareness of our oneness with the Infinite in and as everything and everyone, we bridge the gap between the human and the Divine. Each of us becomes a wise teacher to the world around us by discovering that the two are one.

Express Spiritual Self-Esteem

In his writings about religion, Goethe talked about his conviction that the human soul is indestructible and that its activities will continue through eternity. He likened the soul to the sun, which to our eyes seems to set at night, but has really gone to diffuse its light elsewhere.

Those who make the most of their opportunities in the world of the visible evolve, by way of spiritual self-esteem, to the awareness of the Mystic Mind in action. It is not enough to just know the Truth of our being; we must turn our knowing into wisdom by doing something positive and constructive with it. My friend and mentor Dr. Craig Carter always told me that inspiration is wonderful, but you can easily starve to death while being inspired.

Spiritual self-esteem is the degree we receive from the University of Infinite Intelligence. We begin to light up from within. The loving force of God in all creation becomes visible to us, and we understand more and more of the hidden foundations of the material world.

The one who makes the most of every experience has discovered the human heart is a microcosm of the universal loving heart of God. In his well-known book *The Prophet*, Kahlil Gibran wrote, "You should not say 'God is in my heart, but rather, I am in the heart of God.'" This heart is the life force of all life, which is the body of God everywhere at once.

Spiritual self-esteem is the key to positive self-revelation and interpretation. It may require discipline, teachability, and positive commitment, but the hidden greatness and power we discover in ourselves makes the investment worthwhile. We uncover the treasures within us and put them to use as positive invention, a brilliant, spiritualized intellect, and the heart of a hero. This flames our aspiring soul, and cosmic consciousness becomes our normal way of being.

Spiritual self-esteem is the effect of real self-discovery. In 1 John 3:2, it is written, "Beloved, now are we children of God." We are, right now, what we always have been and shall always be: beloved offspring of the Infinite, through whom eternal Mind expresses itself and its creation.

Whenever we see and understand anything in a clear way, we can never again revert to accepting a vague explanation of it. Only through clear understanding and thinking can we know ourselves as spiritual self-esteem in action. Only through consciously embodying ourselves as such can we function from Love through Law to positive success.

Our enjoyment in our daily tasks—or lack of enjoyment—is only a matter of attitude. Your attitude is a blueprint that the creative energies of the One Mind act upon to unfold as your experience. View every task as a whole wonderful involvement, not merely through the limited confines of your specific duties. Be interested in the overall goals and operations of whatever is being moved forward and being created.

Find enjoyment in performing your work well, and let your self-esteem and efficiency create a happy atmosphere. Be grateful for the opportunity to give the best of yourself to that which is before you, and express the God within you in a beautiful way.

Even though in the past we may have expressed ideas about ourselves as insignificant or secondary, we are all—at this very moment—significant in the Mind of God. When we accept that spiritual self-esteem, as love, is the only real foundation of life, and by living and celebrating all our activities from this realization, everything unlike or contrary to love, health, and happiness is automatically removed from our experience.

Experience Never-Ending Happy Endings

Once upon a time (the story goes), a little girl stood looking at puppies in a pet store, trying to make up her mind which one she would like to take home as a pet. The salesperson, growing impatient, asked if she had finally made up her mind. The child pointed to a puppy that was wagging its tail and stated, "Yes, I want the one with the happy ending."

It would be wonderful if everyone would listen to the clear wisdom of Emerson and others who told us often that we are—or become—what we think about all day long. Wouldn't we then pick only those thoughts that have a happy ending?

We can do this by becoming aware of the Intelligence within us, which affirms that through the operation of the definite Law of Mind, we set into activity all the power we need to produce the good in our experience for which we are willing to pay the price. The price is simply the release of negative insistence; the return is a happy ending.

Knowing this, we realize the problems of yesterday will never show up in our life again—unless we insist on them.

As we study and practice the process of paying the price for health, harmony, and happiness, we discover that our mind is cleared of confusion, and we begin to see and understand the whys and wherefores of our existence. We celebrate the Divine Life in whom we live, move, and have our being. We begin looking for opportunities, celebrating what is right about our thinking, and letting go of worry about the future, our family, our health, and our finances.

With full, positive confidence in ourselves, we find it easy to make intelligent decisions. Knowing this, every answer leads to a new question. We tap into the Creative Principle within our being and learn how to operate and direct it to become our greater good.

By choosing "happy ending" thoughts and ideas, we consciously tap the loving power of the Universe in cooperation with our affirmative right action. We allow our questions and answers to increase our business, improve our grades, restore and maintain our health, and multiply our positive performance everywhere at once.

We become transformed individuals, and amazing achievements become our everyday experience. We remind ourselves that the Infinite Spirit is continuously flowing forth into new expressions through us.

With "happy ending" thinking as our way, we perceive our goals more clearly and pursue the course more diligently. The result is never-ending happy endings.

Capture the Best Prize

We can heal or change anything for the better when our awareness and determination are in the right place. In the beginning, God created us in Its image: perfect. Our awareness of stated perfection is the basis of our new beginning.

Perfection in us, as us, *is* us—and it becomes a new experience of itself as our experience by way of our choice. This is why all the great teachers of every age have taught us to "think about what we think about."

Infinite Spirit is the power that creates all things. We do not of ourselves create; we simply direct creativity by way of our determination. The three steps to being the total embodiment of a Higher Reality are:

1. Know there is a Higher Reality and study the teachers who lived or live there in their own experience.
2. Learn the lesson being taught.
3. Use the lesson we have learned by acting on it and living from it. This is right understanding in action.

At the New York State Fair in 1903, Theodore Roosevelt offered this wisdom to those gathered: "Far and away the best prize life offers is the chance to work hard at work worth doing."

Think about how you work, your friendships, and your relationships with others. We achieve more friendship from others only by learning how to be a better friend to *ourselves* and conducting ourselves in a way that is friendly to the world around us.

We might alter the Golden Rule to remember to do unto *ourselves* as we would have others do unto us. Our friendly behavior will call forth the same attitude of genuine warmth and cordiality in those with whom we share our experience.

True friendship is founded on the basis of *at-one-ment*, the oneness of all people with the One Life of God. Since each person is one with God, everyone is one with everyone else.

The seeds of friendship lie in the hearts of all, awaiting only the warmth of goodwill to bloom forth brighter than ever before. Radiating goodwill to every person you meet—today and every day—is a wonderful way to live.

Infinite Intelligence is everywhere at once. It is the living essence of everything and everyone. It responds to the choosing part of Itself, and we are the part of God that has choice. Spirit creates form from our choice, which becomes our experience. It creates according to our strongest determination. Jesus told us that whoever believes in this Spirit of Life, from within him shall flow springs of living water.

Once we let go and let ourselves discover this truth within, we can never again accept a vague explanation. The God we find within will never again be unknown. Good thinking and good things become our new healthy perception and widen our successful commitment.

Harboring positive opinions becomes a change for the better, without stress. Ernest Holmes, in the very first pages of *Science of Mind*, states that "man, by thinking, can bring into his experience whatsoever he desires—if he thinks correctly, and becomes a living embodiment of his thoughts."

Finding courage, comfort, and joy in celebrating the greatness we know we are allows us to move forward every day with right understanding. Now our determination is in the right place to win the best prize life has to offer.

Activate Positive Self-Awakening

If you have ever felt out of harmony with what was going on around you, let that feeling remind you that it is time to wake up to a greater idea of yourself. Emerson (often called the wisest American, and whose philosophy has informed the life of every New Thought student) believed that a person is truly alive only when he or she becomes a *thinking* person.

We become the amazing power of positive self-awakening in action when we think about what we think about in a self-relying and self-directed way. This means attuning ourselves to the free movement of Supreme Intelligence, which made us out of Itself, and letting It fulfill our every effort. It also means choosing to be in harmony with harmony.

Forever available to us is the creative power to change all our endeavors for the better. As we let go of any misgivings, disappointments, or regrets about any part of our experience that did not meet our expectations, we renew our commitment to being present in this now moment, with a fresh set of self-awakening ideas and new concepts for fulfilling our lives. We allow our highest desires to become our way of life by knowing we have the power to think our way from where we are to where we want to be, and by celebrating what we know we are: a mighty, moving power of God in action.

Our world is rewarding as we let go and allow self-awakening ideas to fill us and enrich everything we think, say and do. Then, we may gratefully celebrate the unlimited possibility of Spirit, which we are, release tension or stress and the reasons for them, and relax into our greater good—awake and aware.

Nothing in the Universe wants us to be unhappy. In *Science of Mind*, Ernest Holmes stated, "We have a right to any happiness of which we can conceive, provided that happiness hurts no one, and is in keeping with the nature of progressive Life."

When we are centered in inner peace, we honor our happiness and let every activity unfold with pleasurable satisfaction. When we are self-awake, we know we are here to love.

Affirm: *I am here to love. I let this Truth by my way!*

Bring Forth the Soul That Makes All

In his poem "The Informing Spirit," Emerson wrote:

> *There is no great and no small*
> *To the Soul that maketh all;*
> *And where it cometh, all things are;*
> *And it cometh everywhere.*

The greatest wisdom of the ages tells us to use our minds to grab hold of our greatest good until it thunders in our world. When we become one with this great vision, we let go of any and all concepts that have kept us from realizing our complete access to the greater good of life.

This includes the acceptance of an abundance of material blessings, new ideas, friendship, love, happiness, and health. This acceptance fulfills itself as our experiences, without delay. Why? Because right action always follows right thinking and believing.

In his poem "Search for Love," D. H. Lawrence wrote:

> *Those that go searching for love*
> *only make manifest their own lovelessness,*
>
> *and the loveless never find love,*
> *only the loving find love,*
> *and they never have to seek for it.*

We always find our self-definition unfolding as our experience. The soul that makes all is love, and every living thing responds to love. Our relationships, home, children, work, and bodies thrive when we embrace everything and everyone with love.

Nothing we do will prosper unless we put our hearts into it. Through positive self-discipline, we can achieve a greater experience of the unlimited spiritual field within. Nothing can hold us in any form of limitation when our identification with the "soul that maketh all" is steadfast and clear.

Chapter Four

The Power of Self-Blessing

The intellect can only take us to the beginning of our process of changing for the better. The secret of moving from the beginning to total embodiment is to spiritualize our intellect. This allows us to demonstrate positive events—greater than anything we have ever known before—in consciousness and experience. I call this flexing our spiritual muscles.

Flex Your Spiritual Muscles

The great Swedish statesman Dag Hammarskjöld said that "life yields only to the conqueror. Never accept what can be gained by giving in. You will be living off stolen goods and your spiritual muscles will atrophy."

It is wonderful what Infinite Intelligence does when called upon. To deeply believe and feel there is One Life, that Life is God, and that Life is our life now is the greatest thing we will ever do for ourselves. This allows us to celebrate the fullness of the indwelling Kingdom and the strength of the Power for Good.

This awareness of Truth opens our unlimited vision as moment by moment we behold the perfect Universe—inwardly and outwardly—and direct our lives to happiness, love, success, prosperity, and mental and physical well-being. Flexing our spiritual muscles inaugurates our daily healthy, stress-free way of being.

The urge of Divine Life in us, as us, is upward, onward, and outward from Itself, through Itself to Itself, by means of everyone, everywhere. As we choose to follow Its course and celebrate Its process as our way, we begin to see clearly that Love is the force of being and that the golden experience of positive progress is ours by right of consciousness.

When we flex our spiritual muscles, we raise our consciousness to a more august level of awareness. As we head in the right direction within our hearts, minds, bodies, and world, positive drive, ambition, and the demand to be the best of ourselves in action become our norm. In return, the world around us begins to give affirmative support that is unparalleled in our personal history.

The process of greater good, getting better all the time, becomes our daily joy as we begin to benefit from acting upon our understanding of these new ideas. Infinite Love is as interested in our success as we are and is always right where we are, moving from consciousness to idea to possibility to mirroring Its absolute Reality as the reality of our experience. When we flex our spiritual muscles, we know without a doubt that something wonderful is happening *now*.

Realize Your Full Potential

Our understanding of the Truth of ourselves will serve us well. If it is not, we must realize that there is more to understand. The Science of Mind teaches not so much that we can get what we want, but that it is within our power to wake up to what we already are. We need not fear the road ahead when we know the truth of ourselves and appreciate that we are a mighty, moving power of intelligent, unlimited potential. When this awakening unfolds as our way of being, we can affirm with confidence daily: *I know where I am going because I know who I am, where I am, and why I am here.*

Our realization of our potential ends self-rejection forever as we practice the Presence of Divine Life in us, as us. Practicing the Presence helps us become aware of our inner intelligence, suspend our judgmental habits of thinking, and let our minds go forth in a celebration of the inspirational wisdom on which we can always draw. This is a process of flowing from thinking about what we are to letting what we are do the thinking.

When we let go and let ourselves trust in Divine Intelligence and accept Its expression in and as our lives, yesterday's problems are healed and resolved, and we are free to move on to greater expressions of Self. Everything that is known is known in Divine Mind, and this is the Mind we use.

The practice of the Presence is a cumulative process and becomes increasingly vivid as we expand our receptivity to it. We can then gratefully accept Divine inspiration wherever we are and practice the Presence in a healthy and beautiful way.

Divine Love made us each out of Itself, so we are important to Life. *I am that which Thou art; Thou art that which I am!* Our awareness that we are wanted, needed, and loved starts with knowing this is true.

The consciousness of belonging to Life and being one with the Divine Presence allows us to realize our potential and accept massive good—expected and unexpected—as our experience. In his book *Know Yourself*, Ernest Holmes stated this truth: "Declare it and decree it, and as surely as the day follows night, shall it dawn upon you through experience, out of practice, that there is a silent Power, actual and dynamic, that heals."

Spiritual perception has always been recognized as freedom from the limitation of world thinking. The Truth in and back of the manifest world of time, space, change, and events is the Reality of Infinite Potential. When we acknowledge the identity of Divine Being as our own identity, unlimited potential unfolds as our lives.

Affirm: *The identity of Divine Being is my true identity. Therefore unlimited potential is unfolding in my life in each and every moment.*

Confident of our oneness with the One, we live every day to the fullest, knowing we have unlimited resources at our command. We use our time lovingly and enthusiastically, thereby adding constructively to our never-ending existence. We are grateful for the deep satisfaction found in our inner realization and awareness of being. Nothing is lost to anxiety, self-doubt, or wishful thinking.

Another day to grow in a positive way becomes our ongoing self-celebration. We know there is no day more important than the one stretching before us right now.

Affirm: *I am a mighty moving power of intelligent, unlimited potential in my world. There is no day more important than the one stretching before me, right now, and I fully embrace this day!*

Fashion Your Life's Beauty

People have difficulty in life not because they want too much, but because they settle for too little. The answer to this difficult situation echoes to us from 3,000 years ago in a declaration of Akhenaten, pharaoh of Egypt in the fourteenth century BC:

Though makest the beauty of form, through thyself alone.
Cities, towns and settlements,
On highway or on river,
All eyes see thee before them,
For thou are Aton [the sun as God] of the day over the earth.

Some people hide in their low self-esteem, doubt, and fear and do not know how to get out. Sometimes our minds are so full of what we do not need to know that we cannot get to what we ought to know. At times the mind is like an attic, cluttered with odds and ends that are useless for generating happiness, success, or greater good. People who will not clean out the attics of their minds go through life as if they were anesthetized above the shoulders. People who do go within to change their thinking let the world see there is no shame in the positive exultation of the Spirit.

Our world is the atmosphere of our thoughts about ourselves—real in its appearance but only an illusion of another reality. The greatest illusion is not the world: we are always our own inventory in action, our own self-definition. There is nothing we have to do. There is nothing we *cannot* do. With God all things are possible.

Our challenge is to use our inventory in an intelligent way, be teachable, and go for the best in a positive way. At this very moment, we all have something within us that has the right intelligent attitude and affirmative awareness about this moment. We will not start to grow in a healthy way until we start to study. If there is pain in our lives, we are off the track.

The great of every age have taught us to speak our word as we want our word to appear. If we conform to the world and let it be our way, we will be living thirdhand; we will exist day after day at the level of an opinion of an opinion. If we let First Cause be our way, we will stop merely existing and will live; we will flow with a Truth that knows no opposite. This experience is a "swift kick in the can'ts."

The lesson is to discover how to direct our emotions and enjoy the healthy functions of our bodies and world. We love God's humanity, to which we all belong, cultivating habits that bring progress and prosperous unfoldment. We lovingly do unto everyone that which we would have them do unto us. We are optimistic, breathing the atmosphere of cheerfulness, and it is wonderful.

Seize Extraordinary Opportunities

In these fast-moving times, every man, woman, boy, and girl needs a massive dose of spiritual self-awareness, intelligent self-esteem, healthy self-respect, and successful self-direction. If we are in a climate of doubt, fear, or competition but truly desire to demonstrate our own highest goals, we can become one with the lessons of Science of Mind and realize our own potential for health, wealth, and happiness. And we can let it happen now.

Every exploration into the Science of Mind teaching is an extraordinary opportunity because it offers lessons we all need and can use now. These lessons are accompanied by a principle that is only limited by our imagination. Everyone who applies these lessons to his or her life is privileged to witness the power and the impact of this wonderful teaching we call Science of Mind.

Directing our life experiences in a positive way becomes our "standard normal" as we discover the finest truth about ourselves and learn how to work what the world calls "the miraculous" in our lives. We improve our minds and lovingly unleash the power for healthy greatness within us. Resounding success becomes our every experience as we let go and let Infinite Intelligence accelerate the good in our lives—the good that is ours by right of consciousness.

When we learn how to be happy and successful, everyone prospers. When we direct our life experiences in a healthy-minded way, we daily realize great improvement in every area of our lives, and we are confident in our ability to succeed. We are eager to learn and grow from lessons of the great, the good, and the wise, and we let our highest ideals become our ideas and our way. We find a lesson in every experience, apply the lesson to our lives as wisdom, and evolve as an example of positive self-renewal.

The importance of positive self-renewal in all aspects of our lives is evident in the work of John W. Gardner, founder of Common Cause, an organization promoting good government. He believed that self-renewal is needed both by the nation and by those who desire to fight off stagnation. This is worth thinking about as we sit down by ourselves for a quiet time of Spiritual Mind Treatment, intelligent positive thinking, and quality self-evaluation about who we are, what we are doing, why we are doing it, and where we are going. This frees us to accept the greater good and more abundant living that accompanies the unfolding of our positive purpose.

Believe That You Receive

There is a statement attributed to Jesus (Mark 11:24) that "all things whatsoever ye pray and ask for, believe that ye receive them, and ye shall have them." This declaration has engendered more enlightenment in the heart, mind, and life of the metaphysical student than perhaps any other statement of Truth.

In his book *Being and Becoming*, Fenwicke Holmes put it this way: "If I can know anything at all, I can know I am. If I can know I am, I can know that I think. If I can know I think, I can depend upon the sanity or reasonableness of my thinking."

Here is a question we should all ask ourselves: *is what I think* really *what I think?* We are what we think about all day long, but we are not restricted to yesterday's thought or experience. We can renew our mind and thinking at any moment. The Power that created us out of Itself creates our experience based on the pattern we give to It by way of our belief. If our world is not as happy, healthy, and abundant as we know it can be, it is not because we do not believe; it is because we believe in the wrong thing.

We can always let a change for the better become our reality by knowing we are already a perfect idea in the Mind of God, made in the image of Divine greatness. In this awareness, we can choose to be wise self-thinkers and follow an inner positive plan for successful living. We discover ourselves loving life more and enjoying every moment of it in new and wonderful ways. We begin to celebrate how easy it is to devote ourselves to never-ending self-improvement and the betterment of our world.

This kind of experience happens every time we let go and let ourselves be the consciousness of God in action. Our body and world change instantly for the better with every positive change we make in our inner expression. When we change our belief, we change ourselves and change the conditions around us.

If there is ever any fear or doubt, all we have to do is remember to feel the conviction and belief that the Power that created us out of Itself has all the health, supply, and answers we could ever want or need. It is Divine Mind's good pleasure to give to Itself as us by way of our belief.

Affirm: *The Power that created me out of Itself has all the health, supply, and answers I could ever want or need. It is God's good pleasure to give to Itself—as me— by way of my belief.*

Establish Focused Faith

The metaphysical meaning of the word *concentration* takes on new understanding when we see it in its true light. *Concentration* is a word derived from two Latin roots: *con-*, a prefix meaning *with*, and *centrum*, meaning *center* or *fixed central point*. The two words combined literally mean, *to bring to a common point, to focus.* So the word *concentration* means *the act or state of bringing to a fixed point or focus.*

The amount of good we accept depends entirely upon the size of our concept of God, for It does the measuring. Rev. H. E. Fosdick took the stance that when a man says he can get on without religion, it merely means he has a kind of religion he can get on without.

Our challenge is to enlarge our concept of the Power that created us out of Itself and focus our expanded concept on our experience. God is inborn in all of us. It is always ready to change our lives for the better and heal our difficulties.

As we focus by way of positive faith in our oneness with God, all things come to pass. When we focus our thinking, we better our thoughts. As we direct our thoughts from Truth to experience, we mold our circumstances. The way to successful living is focused faith.

Ernest Holmes referred to focused faith as "the substance of things hoped for; the evidence of things not seen" (see Hebrews 11:1).

Simplify Spiritual Courage

It does not take a metaphysician to understand the simplicity of spiritual courage. To believe a healthier, happier self is good enough to be true, and to prepare for it, gives it permission to give birth to itself as our experience.

This principle appeals to all thinking people. A genuine optimism pervades our life—a fellowship with God, whose course is our common share of the Great Life that is forever given to the Universe.

The Greek philosopher Heraclitus believed that wisdom is the oneness of mind that guides and permeates all things.

We are all flowing through the adventure of life, and there is no reason it should not be an enjoyable trip.

Our personal story deserves to be one of spiritual courage lovingly touching the heart of our world. Anyone can worry, be afraid, or feel unhappy. It does not take one ounce of intelligence to be negative. Likewise, anyone can discover the place, power, and charm of Light thinking and spiritual awareness to make this a better world to live in.

There comes a time when it is wise to stop dreaming and discover the divine charm at the center of our being, becoming a blessing in our own lives. The time is now!

Chapter Five

Move into Active Acceptance of Your Divine Good

Many people today are confused about their place in Divine Mind and Divine Mind's place in them. Einstein stated: "The number one question in the mind of the human being is, 'Is the Universe friendly?'" The answer to this question is yes. Allow me to explain.

Focus Your Infinite Individualized Attention

When we focus our infinite individualized attention on our health, happiness, and prosperity, we are aligning with the great wisdom of Deuteronomy 6:4: "Hear, O Israel: Jehovah our God is one Jehovah."

Metaphysically understood, this means "Comprehend and appreciate (hear), enlightened human mind that is spiritually awake within us (O Israel): the ultimate Intelligent Power that is everywhere at once (Jehovah), the Divine Mind of us (our God), is the one force of the Infinite."

To put it plainly: there is no such thing as the Infinite *and* something else.

The Infinite moves through our individualized attention and fulfills Itself as our experience. This is the principle of the Infinite in action, and it operates through us, in us, and as us, whether we know it or not. As we become aware of the Infinite moving from Itself, through Itself, to Itself as our experience, we allow unbridled positive enthusiasm to evolve our world and run away with our healthy imagination.

Here is what I advise for new students and long-time students of the wonderful art of practicing infinite individualized attention:

1. Know there is always more to know.
2. Be teachable and patient. When we let go of the old and set the new in motion, our world can sometimes become crazy. (Remember we have to stay a little crazy to remain sane!)
3. Know that the flab of fad metaphysics will often hide the Truth. What we know, we do. Everything else is just theory.
4. Capture the wisdom and essence of everything we have experienced, and welcome growth and change.
5. Know there is no such thing as coincidence.
6. Know that "God gave us not a spirit of fearfulness; but of power and love and discipline" (2 Timothy 1:7).

All who listen to this advice celebrate our choice to do so. Letting the power of this Truth be our way allows us to expect positive answers about our health, wealth, and relationships. We move forward in life as acceptance in action, knowing that no matter how limited our situation may seem, there is nothing that Principle, operating through infinite individualized attention, cannot solve. As we place our confidence in this power outside of ourselves, we become grateful for the important part we each play in the greatness of life; we appreciate our daily manifestation and everyone in it.

See with Divine Wisdom

If we trust in the Divine Presence and surrender to It when we feel doubt and fear, our negative point of view begins to evaporate, and the wisdom within unfolds as a new, healthy perspective. We find it easy to depend only on the indwelling Divine Presence and not upon person, place, or thing. Spirit guides our thinking, and ideas of greater good flow freely through our minds. Free from adverse thought, we know we are steadfast and unwavering in our acceptance of Divine Action.

As we speak from the perspective of wisdom, our harvest will be infinite; our words will not come back to us void. We grow in freedom and understanding of the true quality of existence. As we read in Romans 12:2, "Be ye transformed by the renewing of your mind."

Constant endeavor and vision are necessary to achieve consistent direction of conscious thought. Perhaps in the past we have been muddled, worried, apprehensive and discouraged, causing unhappy conditions. If this has been so, it is now time to change the patterns of thinking.

By exchanging a positive attitude for a depressed one—not at some future time, but right now—we establish the foundation of better things to come. It is important to handle each moment and master every situation immediately. Ernest Holmes emphasized this by teaching, "That which thought has done, thought can undo." He firmly believed that lifelong habits of wrong thinking can be consciously and deliberately neutralized, and an entire new order of mental and emotional reactions can be established in Mind.

When we open our hearts and minds to wisdom, we let the indwelling Spirit flow forth through us in harmonious relation with our world and everyone in it. When by conscious direction of thought we let wisdom be our viewpoint, we form new and constructive patterns and change apparent defeat into victory. This moves us in consciousness into joy and peace, a state that reflects itself in all we contact and in everything we do.

By our own living, we can impart to the world around us the concept of using Divine Wisdom as our perspective. God expresses in us as right thinking and manifests as health and harmony, love and kindness, and objectivity and devotion. By listening to the indwelling Spirit of Wisdom, and by following Its lead, each of us has an invincible authority for good and can light the way for more. We are the mighty moving power of God in our world.

Affirm: *I am the mighty moving power of God in my world.*

Get What You Ought to Want

Theologian Edgar S. Brightman taught a great lesson in wisdom. Brightman believed that the practical man is the man who knows how to get what he wants; the philosopher is the man who knows what man ought to want; the ideal man is the man who knows how to get what he ought to want.

How do we let ourselves be the ideal person, letting our *ideal* become our *idea* and demonstrating everything that fulfills our highest concept of good? How do we become more than a *student* of Divine Principle and become a *disciple* of Divine Principle?

The first step is to accept that God, Infinite Mind, is the omnipresent Principle that lives, moves, and has Its being as us. It is the Good that works in, through, and for Itself—as us. As the Bible states (John 4:24), "God is a Spirit; and they that worship him must worship him in spirit and in truth."

The second step can be defined as divine or positive perseverance. This is the moment-by-moment, day-by-day appreciation of the Divine Presence unfolding as our experience. It is discovering the courage, comfort, and joy within and letting it come forth as full consciousness.

The third step occurs as our perceptions widen in a positive way. Our understanding, opinions, and ideas change for the better. We know that what God *is* exists here and now, and whatever we need to know is no longer unknown. We are prepared to surrender to health, happiness, and harmony, and we do so with love. We let go and let the goodness of the great ideas manifest outwardly.

As we move through this third step, we release any interest in the negative. Our limited estimation of ourselves and our world fades, and our curious mind delights in knowing what it never knew before. We awaken to our Divine Power, put our successful ambition in gear, and soar in contemplating the essence of knowledge and the experience of wisdom.

We are Intelligence, Life, and Love concentrated into one drop of precious Truth in the whole stream of existence. When we know the Mind that thinks, the Power that knows, the Intelligence that creates, and the Wisdom that directs us *are* the vibrant life forces of our being, we know how to get what we ought to want.

Affirm: *All that I desire and need to know is no longer unknown to me. I surrender to health, happiness, and harmony with love and gratitude.*

Act as Infinite Love

In *The Science of Successful Living*, Raymond Charles Barker often affirmed for himself that God "loves the world by means of me!" We make this our experience when we understand the Principle and Power of Love and Law in Action, and think as It thinks, give as It gives, and act as It acts.

Ernest Holmes believed that everyone thinks, but few think about what they think about. As students of Science of Mind, we learn not to believe everything we think. Through this awakening, we discover how to grasp things effortlessly— even ideas.

Change is inevitable. The progressive, loving, and happy person is the one who quickly adjusts to and celebrates change. Those who look at their day and see nothing but the uncertainty of change tend to react impulsively, without due mindfulness. If we observe ourselves resenting a person, place, or idea, we need to take time to contemplate its true value; otherwise, we are unknowingly resisting and resenting our own greater good.

When we fail to understand that the Infinite Life is a God of Law as well as a God of Love, we accept the judgments of the world, and we rebel against what seems to be arbitrary. Rather than embracing the Law, we judge according to appearances.

The clearest minds of every age have taught that when we know what and who we are, we can move through anything and be unmoved by it. When we know what and who we are, our way becomes Love in action, without effort. The creative Law of Love is infinite; It always demonstrates perfection in our lives.

When we choose to think as Divine Love thinks, we know that our thought is made manifest in a perfect demonstration of success, harmony, and health. Whatever belongs to us as Love in action must unfold in our individual lives. This is true because Infinite Intelligence is compelled to recognize our good and see, understand, accept, and express more by means of Itself as us.

Such awareness stays with us as we remind ourselves that we are made in the image and likeness of the One Love, and we are each an individual display of cosmic consciousness. Two thousand years ago, the lesson came forth that we should seek first the kingdom of God and God's righteousness (Matthew 6:33), and all other things will be added unto us. Believe that this is good enough to be true, and let Love be your way.

Become Awareness in Motion

In Romans 1:20–21, we discover that ever since God created the world, his invisible, everlasting power and deity have been clearly seen and understood, so even people in those times had no excuses. They knew God and yet refused to honor Him as God or thank Him. Instead, they made nonsense out of logic, and their empty minds were darkened so they could not understand.

Awareness has no other way to appear than when we let it appear. Life, and what we represent in it, can be summed up in this idea: it is as if God Itself does not know what is going to happen in the next moment until that moment is here. Each of us is being what we think about at every moment with body, mind, and spirit—and that is enough.

Every moment of time—not yet here, not yet lived, not yet expressed—holds the possibility of everything in its mystery. In the realm of the unknown, anything and everything is truly possible, even things we have not yet thought of. We can imagine our lives, from the things we fear to the things we love, and all is possible. Why? Because life is so vast, so far beyond human comprehension, that *anything* can take place as our experience.

It's up to each of us to embrace the directive to "be transformed by the renewing of your mind." As we let our minds move from what we feel and think, we need to ask ourselves, "What is important to me, both as an individual and as part of the Universe—the totality of all things that exist?"

As we expand into universal wisdom, we develop an awareness of the omnipresence, omniscience, and omnipotence of Spirit. We are a part of the One Mind.

As we let our minds move from what we feel to what we think to what we know is important to us, we free ourselves to use universal wisdom. We know the importance of individual imagination, out of which comes the definitions of consciousness, fear, dreams, nightmares, and revelations.

True awareness lets us know that we can always put Universal Love into our thoughts in place of any fear, doubt, or limited idea. This makes us powerful. We are not dealing with a special, abstract power. We are dealing with the awareness that we are part of the Magnificent Presence. We are the very Creative Source of the Universe.

Jesus said we are the children of God; it's the Father's good pleasure to give us the Kingdom, and we are to always remember that it is done unto us as we believe.

Cultivate Common Sense

Common sense used in an uncommon way must unfold as uncommon results. One person gets nothing but discord from the strings of a guitar; another gets harmony. No one would claim the guitar is at fault.

Life and living offer the same experience. Disharmony may exist, but so does harmony. Common sense tells us that like the guitar, life, played correctly—from the positive—gives forth the beautiful. Play it in a false or negative way, and it will give forth the ugly. Life is not at fault.

Ernest Holmes explained his thoughts on common sense in *The Anatomy of Healing Prayer*. He said that Religious Science is nothing more than common sense, adding, "God knows that common sense is the most uncommon thing in the world."

An unusual amount of common sense is defined as wisdom. Wisdom is nothing more than common sense refined by doing, learning, and experiencing.

When we learn to live, we will live to learn. To take a page from the Greek dramatist Euripides: "If youth and age came twice . . . we could set things right, no matter what mistakes were made."

To be of the greatest value, one's religion should be intellectually sound, spiritually enlightened, emotionally satisfying, and centered in common sense. The phrase "let the mind be in you which was also in Christ Jesus" (Philippians 2:5) points toward a mental reconditioning, a reeducation of the self from common sense, and a remaking of our life experiences for the better.

Humorist Will Rogers quipped that "there is more need today for common sense than at any time since people stopped having a lot of it." As metaphysicians, we have the power to correct this.

Do Common Things in Uncommon Ways

We can attain a greater understanding of the wonder of ourselves and our immense power for health, wealth, and happiness when we see ourselves as part of a developing Universe.

Booker T. Washington, president and principal developer of what is now Tuskegee University, often lectured on how people prosper by learning to do common things in an uncommon way. He would often say, "Cast down your buckets where you are."

We let down the bucket where we are when we wake up to the truth of what is written in 2 Timothy 1:7: "For God hath not given us the spirit of fear; but of power, and of love, and of a sound mind." When we approach life with this type of sound mind, our lives are always God's Life, and God's Life always prospers.

In his essay "The Over-Soul," Emerson summed it up perfectly when he wrote that if a man "has found his home in God, his manners, his forms of speech, the turn of his sentences, the build . . . of his opinions, will involuntarily confess it."

As we let each ending be a beginning and build stronger, higher, and happier goals for ourselves, we achieve those goals (and more) with ease. Our ideals become our ideas and come into full expression.

The Roman philosopher Seneca shared that no matter how rich a soil may be, it cannot be productive without culture; similarly, a mind without cultivation can never produce good fruits. Our challenge is to discover the gift each of us is, open it, and give it to our world with love.

Chapter Six

The Power of
Spiritual Willingness

As we unlimit our understanding of the Truth of our being, we discover we are merged with the Universal Spirit. It is in us as we are in It. The same nature, in an apparently different ratio.

When we wake up and realize the only thing in our way is "our way," we discover the wisdom of God in us, as us, everywhere at once. It knows what to do and how to do it. Ernest Holmes summed up this idea in *Richer Living*: "The 'skillful masters' who have penetrated the mystery of life which so often eludes the intellect, are those who with utmost simplicity have found direct approach to the supreme reality at the center of their own soul."

Become a Brave, Determined Spirit

A brave, determined spirit is ours when we let go and become one with what the clear thinkers of every age have called the unerring judgment of Divine Intelligence. This is the truth of every religion, but it is not religion that makes it true.

According to Mark Twain, "The miracle or the power that elevates the few is to be found in their industry, application and perseverance under the promptings of a brave, determined spirit." Our challenge is to be brave enough to embody the reality of Principle—that Divine Mind is everywhere at once—and let the world see we know that with God, all things are possible.

When we allow ourselves to be brave, determined Spirit in action, we know that our goals, desires, and the Divine Urge, properly nourished, become positive fulfillment. A change in thinking for the better always brings about renewed health, harmony, and happiness. Without stress, our dreams of success and prosperity become our reality.

As Jesus was recorded to have told the centurion, who firmly believed that the power of the spoken word could set things right, "as thou hast believed, so be it done unto thee" (Matthew 8:13). Belief must be refined and acted upon, and anything antagonistic to it must be released. We do not have to know *how* something is going to happen, as long as we are committed to our objective.

If we conceive of the idea, the whole of Universal Intelligence moves upon Itself as us, and completes the idea in our life. Divine Mind knows exactly what to do, as well as how, when, and where to do it—when we let go and let it be so.

Let us each remind ourselves that positive self-discipline and a passion for living obliterate every bit of confusion and discord. When we choose to be one with the spirit of brave determination, we free ourselves from the boundaries of yesterday, discover the higher reaches of consciousness, and grow in the fullness of Divine Principle and Divine Purpose.

Undertake Greater Things

The grand and vivid thinkers of every age have told us that the Truth and Principle of Infinite Intelligence is the Truth and Principle of our being. When we know this, and know we know it, we are able to live our lives and love what we are choosing to do with them. Our daily affirmation becomes, *I am here. It is now. I am alive, and I matter.*

Intelligence, teachability, and positive experimentation in the face of everyday experience are invitations to unlimited success. Each of us is the unlimited power of positive Principle in action. As we direct our lives from this awareness, we rid our experience of risk and let affirmative certainty be our way. Explosive happiness, unequivocal power, and confident commitment are required in the presence of Life, which is heaven-bent on healthy unfoldment.

In the experience of living and loving from Principle, one rule applies: "Do unto others as you would have others do unto you." Then we are subject to an attack of greatness, and abundant good fills our lives from unexpected people, places, and things—from anyone, anywhere, and anything. We discover the ability to celebrate even the slightest opportunity to realize our good.

When we become one with the Reality of Principle, we free ourselves of stinking thinking and see that greater health, abundance, happiness, and good are lovingly unavoidable. Our positive responsiveness allows the entire situation to be better and better. Stinking thinking never changed anyone's life for the better, but confident thinking and endeavor will demonstrate the wonderful, everywhere at once. Confident thinking requires mastery of the Truth of Self. The American philosopher Elbert Hubbard believed that the reason we do not *accomplish* greater things is that we do not *undertake* greater things.

When the Reality of Principle is our way, we undertake greater things and discover we are fanning the spark of Divine Urge into a brightly burning flame within our hearts. This kind of self-discovery guarantees success—the greatest adventure of all—because we are working in harmony with the great spiritual Principle of the Universe. Our lives become a feast of marvels, our demonstrations are dazzling, and we understand the Infinite as never before.

At the core of human experience is the heart and the mind; at the core of both heart and mind is Principle. The search for Infinite Intelligence in a Divine Universe leads to awareness, for as Ernest Holmes taught us: "What we are searching *for*, we are searching *with*." We become tireless proponents of our positive spiritual heritage.

Embrace Positive Self-Discovery

Our challenge is to evolve in our process of positive self-discovery and live in a clear, discerning, and healthy way in the present. It is up to each of us to experiment, research, and experience the higher Truth of Life and actively participate in the greater good as our mind, body, and world. Only by doing so will we truly understand the joy of living—not as the world knows it, but as Divine Mind knows it.

The valuable lessons of metaphysics become intelligible and fulfilling in our lives only when we live from them and become the process of positive self-discovery in action. This process is not an end to itself, but the essential means of personal growth and awareness. This is inner and outer research into the Truth of infinite freedom. We must naturally and effectively let the action of our understanding be the wonder of our way.

The committed student of New Thought will spend her lifetime studying, understanding, and developing the all-encompassing experience and art of metaphysics as a way of life. Ernest Holmes affirmed this concept, believing that whatever is ideal must also be practical. Whatever is heaven must also be earth; whatever is Divine must at the same time be human. Unless every part of the Universe is some part of Reality, there is Reality, and then there is something else.

Truth is universal, and every teacher points to the Truth. Truth is not Truth if it is leading us to something or someone other than our true Self.

All our dreams are waiting for us to come true, relative to them. The best idea in the Universe cannot do anything *for* us unless we let it *be* us. The rewards of letting this awareness be our way are enormous, and our sense of well-being and self-esteem begins to flourish as never before.

Author Ralph Waldo Trine shared this lesson in *Through the Sunlit Year*: "It's the duty and it should be the pleasure of each while here to think bravely and to live bravely straight through to the end. It's the manly and the womanly thing to do—and besides it pays. To take captive the best things in life we must proceed always through the channel of brave, intrepid thought."

Relax and Celebrate

We become better persons by using our divine capabilities. As a result, our world becomes a better place in which to live.

The ability to "let go and let God" opens new roads to health, success, and happiness. Letting go and letting God opens the mind and heart to all that Infinite Mind has to offer us. The kingdom of God is truly within us, as us. Therefore, our thoughts and feelings must be relaxed, stress-free, and receptive to inner peace, joy, health, security, and order if we are to realize such good in our lives. This is the way to inherit the kingdom.

When we feel life is a weight and the burden is too heavy, the result is strain. This brings the feeling of powerlessness, of being unequal to the responsibility of it all.

Many of us fall into this type of thinking simply because we struggle to overcome human tendencies. To the contrary, we can celebrate tension-free living, using these five steps:

1. **Completely relax.** We underestimate our inner strength and resourcefulness for applying spiritual methods to worldly problems. People do not really know what they are capable of until they completely relax. Yet time and again, we have observed how far we exceed ourselves whenever we express a relaxed state of mind in meeting the demands made upon us. Our potential is endless.

2. **Be the vigor of mind in action.** I have heard it said that the mind is like a bow: it is the stronger for being unbent. A good archer never stretches his or her bow beyond its strength for the control and accuracy desired. As soon as the archer reaches that point, he or she returns it to a relaxed position. So it is in our thinking. No one can be a bent bow all the time! If we are, people will surely comment, "If only they would unbend a little!"

3. **Practice relaxed conversation.** In today's fast-moving society, too many of us occasionally fit the description of the Red Queen in *Alice's Adventures in Wonderland*, who had to keep running all the time just to stand still. Nothing betrays an unrelaxed mind so much as frantic dialogue. We need to practice relaxed conversation to receive the right responses from others. The prize of pure communication will not be a celebration unless it is released from strain and anxiety. Just think of a tight rosebud. Could it ever bloom without going through a phase of relaxation in the growth process, each petal unfolding gently by itself? Apply the power to have time for yourself, and you hold the reins of life in your hand.

4. **Relax your breath of life.** Relaxation is as essential to our well-being and spiritual growth as breathing, eating, and sleeping are to our physical health. When we relax, we get our best ideas and deepest insights for happy, successful living. The subconscious works more efficiently through a relaxed conscious mind. When we grow still and let go of tense personal thoughts, there is a beneficial response from our inner self.

This means relaxation is not complete until our world itself is relaxed and an inner freedom from strain, pressure, and tension is achieved.

5. **Release the need to control.** Letting go and letting God is how we inherit the kingdom of God within. We are one with Universal Mind, and our thought is creative. We think only good in order that we may express good. We do not make something happen; the Law of our being creates through the paradigm of our thought.

We use this power every time we think. As we let Infinite Mind express Itself in us, as us, we permit only joy, happiness, and successful achievement to manifest in our experience. Our thought partakes of the Nature of God, and our life becomes an ever fuller expression of heaven on earth. When we practice positive relaxation, increased health, happiness, and harmony flow from the spiritual movement of life within us.

Knowledge must be put into action. By thinking in terms of health, wise and loving action, and abundant good for ourselves and others, we contribute to a better world.

Build More Stately Mansions

In what kind of Universe do we live, move, and have our being? What is the Universe's purpose, form, and nature? It is the creation of Infinite Love. The Universe is Infinite Life. Life lived from love is celebration, a solvable mystery, and a process of growth.

The word *life* implies healthy growth. When any person, place, or thing refuses to grow, it begins to recede, decay, and die. This truth applies not only to the life experience, but also to business, government, and the world itself. Positive self-image promotes positive imagination, which gives birth to new ideas, which in turn bring healthy growth and change. This is what Oliver Wendell Holmes was describing in his poem "The Chambered Nautilus": "Build thee more stately mansions, O my soul, / As the swift seasons roll!"

The stately mansions are the higher levels of consciousness and awareness. The swift seasons represent the Divine Urge as Intuition, flowing through us ceaselessly as thought, idea, and feeling. This is the creation of Infinite Love in action. Its purpose is to celebrate Its own perfection and show it forth.

The wonderful truth about perfection is that it does not care what we do with it. We can be perfectly happy or perfectly unhappy, perfectly sick or well, perfectly abundant or broke. Its form is our body, world, and experience. Its nature is to turn into form by way of our consciousness.

Our challenge is to let go and let our good happen. How do we get ourselves out of the way to do this, to move forward as this idea? The first steps are to let go and let love be our advancing front edge, understanding that we are unlimited expressions of Life in action.

There is no limit to what we are. We have the ability, the power, and the beauty within us to heal anything in our lives that needs to be healed and to change anything that needs to change for the better.

It is written that Jesus told his disciples (John 14:3) that he came to go before us to prepare a place for us. Think about this idea as a state of consciousness, a state of being. Every thought we embody goes before us and prepares a place for us, and—count on it—we are going to move into it and live in it. This is why we need to be responsible for what we are accepting as ourselves and our experience.

Ernest Holmes taught that inspiration without application is hallucination. Let us each do something wonderful with our inspiration and bless our world by way of our choices. Let us reject ideas of unreason or injustice, and let our hearts be open to the joys of Infinite Love. Let us welcome Spirit into our lives and minds with all our being, spectacularly, for then Spirit shall truly find a more stately mansion.

Cultivate Spectacular Thinking

Our challenge is to go to the place within—the silence, the canvas on which anything can be expressed—and ask ourselves, "How does the spectacular awareness of the Thing Itself (mystic Reality) lead us to think, live, move and have our being as It?" Then we let the answer that comes to us become our way.

People need myths because they think Truth is less spectacular. In actuality, the Truth embodied becomes spectacular beyond definition.

Affirm: *I now think about the spectacular until I think as the spectacular.*

Remember, we can always trust the Universe regarding the path to our individual positive purpose. We can start by putting the mystical Reality of God Itself into perspective in order to celebrate our spectacular awareness of Oneness. When we do this, we align our thinking with the wisdom of Emerson in his essay "Spiritual Laws": "There is one direction in which all space is open to [man]. He has faculties silently inviting him thither to endless exertion. He is like a ship in a river; he runs against obstructions on every side but one: on that side all obstruction is taken away and he sweeps serenely over a deepening channel into an infinite sea."

That channel is God's depths. The only way to have a spectacular life is by way of spectacular thinking. Then we will sweep serenely over limitation, doubt, and fear into Infinite Possibility.

Recognize the Winner in Everyone

The greatness of God is everything. As we become aware of this Truth, we clearly understand that everyone is a winner.

Knowing this, we choose to work hard every day to be the best we can be in everything we think, say, and do. This is serving our purpose of being with love.

The more we know we are the power of the Infinite in action, the more we are on top of everything in our experience. Why? Because we each project what happens in our world, and when we love it, our projection is wonderful. We move forward each moment affirming, "I succeed because I am a success!" This is the celebration of the healing power within us that is cause to our positive growth.

We have the right to experience the consciousness of money as the result of giving positive support as our commitment to Life. We have the right to love and be loved as the effect of our oneness with healthy expansion.

The implications for our intelligent evolution are immeasurable. By way of Infinite Mind—in us and as us—we celebrate our power to direct our life and determine our experience, and we manifest as winners.

Every day, we can let go and let greater good make a successful, spontaneous appearance in our life. Let us greet it with joy.

Affirm: *Every day, I let go and let greater good make a successful, spontaneous appearance in my life. I succeed because I am a success.*

Chapter Seven

The Power of You

W hen we wake up to the realization that *all* of Divine Principle is right where we are, fulfilling our belief, we discover we are always at the top of our positive game plan. We find ourselves climbing the never-ending peak of unlimited success. We end our thinking from yesterday's awareness and become *now* thinkers. We are one with the age-old truth that God, Divine Intelligence, is everywhere at once. All time is *now*. Everything that has been and everything that will be is happening at once. God has evolved and individualized each one of us out of Itself; therefore, we are all the embodiment of everything positive and wonderful about life and living. We are God's total package.

Our philosophical exploration into the idea of the continual unfolding of intelligent love frees us to discover the difference between health-producing and disease-producing ideas.

Choose health, and let it become the power of positive leverage in the unlimited opportunity of living from Principle.

The same understanding and approach to life that was the light and the way of the great and wise of every age can be the heart of our success in every area of our lives. This frees us to celebrate the enormous reserves of natural intelligence, talent, and creativity within us. We find ourselves opting not to coast along on our God-given abilities. We always receive what we give, multiplied.

Since change is the only thing in the Universe that is constant, the greatest speed in shifting our thinking for the better becomes of utmost importance. Divine Principle frees us to fill our minds with unlimited combinations of healthy, prosperous ideas.

Everything in our experience is constantly moving from where it has been to where it can be, by means of us. As we grow into a greater understanding, we relax into greater good. At the same time, we strengthen our minds, our bodies, and our world. In this way, we are constantly improving our grip on positive self-discipline and letting intelligent self-definition be our advancing edge.

Through our own choice of thought, we cause people, things, and events to become what they are *to us*. If we think a thing is real, it is real in our experience. Likewise, if we refuse to accept or recognize the need for any detrimental condition, it cannot continue to exist for us.

As the total package of God, we have within ourselves the power to choose what we think. Therefore we can allow our world to be anything we want it to be. As Proverbs 23:7 says about man: "As he thinks in his heart, so is he."

Affirm: *I refuse to accept or recognize the need for any detrimental condition. No such limitation exists for me or anyone else.*

Build Intelligent Self-Esteem

One great effect in the life of the metaphysician is intelligent self-esteem. Indeed, there is nothing more fundamental in this rapidly changing world of ours than the need for intelligent self-esteem.

A person who abides in a state of self-doubt, self-deprecation, or self-distrust is standing in his or her own way when facing the ongoing challenges of living. A healthy understanding that God expresses Itself by means of us leads us to self-reliance, self-respect, and self-trust. This awareness must be actualized if we are going to fulfill our lives with health, success, and love.

Why do people withhold greater good from their own lives? It is because they do not comprehend and embody the idea that we live from a limitless source of never-ending good. Henry David Thoreau summed it up by saying, "The mass of men lead lives of quiet desperation." He also advised that the answer to this negative experience is to "enter the heaven of self-realization."

To get our self-esteem in gear and derive more from our living experience, we must continually give more of our positive self. By doing this, we lovingly discover the esteem of God as our exhaustless Self.

As we give of our riches, our abundance increases. As we give of our joy, understanding, and love, we find ourselves meeting these same qualities, which bless, enrich, and heal our lives and world. Being one in consciousness with the esteem of God and letting It unfold as intelligent self-esteem is indispensable, not only to our healthy well-being, but to our daily participation in the process of living.

When we let self-respect be our way, we find our capacity to respect others. When we experience a deep sense of security and self-trust, we begin to contribute to the world and all the people in it in great and wonderful ways. People who have experienced clear self-awareness and have allowed it to evolve into positive self-love have a great capacity to experience the love of others.

This is God expressing as our intelligent self-esteem in action. If we choose to let this lesson be our way, we will congratulate ourselves forever for making the choice.

Up the Ante of Your Life Experience

Back in 1991, when Pat Riley took over as head coach for the New York Knicks, he determined that his team that season would have only one goal: to become the hardest-working team in the NBA. He didn't know if that goal would translate into wins but believed this is where you start. Challenging his team to meet this goal was, in his opinion, nothing more than upping the ante.

We up the ante of our experience when we commit ourselves to being the best students we can be, being unending teachability in action. This is the real meaning of the biblical statement, "Blessed are the meek, for they shall inherit the earth" (Matthew 5:5). The meek are the teachable. Fenwicke Holmes believed that the best teacher is one who teaches in such a way that his students can replace him. Every good teacher celebrates every student who chooses to be part of this positive growth experience.

We roll away the stone of ignorance and move into the light of self-realization when we discover within ourselves the great faculty of affirmative embodiment and use it wisely. As we open our eyes to the Truth, we know we are not bound by any of the false concepts we have observed in our world.

We each have within us the power to learn whatever we need to learn to rise above all negation and stand firm in positive faith. Abraham Lincoln affirmed for himself that he would study and prepare for a career in law on his own and that someday he would become a lawyer. And he did.

Years later, Lincoln received a letter from a young man who wondered if he would take him under his tutelage, as (like in Lincoln's case) there were no law teachers near him. Lincoln politely declined but advised the youth to "always bear in mind that your own resolution to success is more important than any other one thing." That young man was Isham Reavis, whose resolution to succeed led him to become an associate justice of the Arizona Supreme Court.

Along a similar vein, famed German mystic Meister Johannes Eckhart declared that "to get at the core of God at His greatest, one must first get into the core of himself at his least, for no one can know God who has not first known himself. Go to the depths of the soul, the secret place of the Most

High, to the roots, to the heights; for all that God can do is focused there."

The mystic minds of the ages have all known what the Apostle Paul reminded us: "In Him we live, and move, and have our being" (Acts 17:28). Most people are gasping at life like a fish out of water, although what they need for sustenance and healthy development is around them all the time.

"No man can reveal to you aught but that which already lies half asleep in the dawning of your knowledge," wrote Kahlil Gibran in *The Prophet*. By way of intelligent religion, we can each underscore God's gift to Itself, as us, and demonstrate through our creative abilities a greatness beyond anything we have known before.

In his essay "Immortality," Emerson declared that "learning depends on the learner. No more truth can be conveyed than the popular mind can bear." Ernest Holmes advised his students to embrace the truth he himself had discovered: that "the more I know, the more I know there is more to know."

Let us each up our ante and use our intelligence and talents for the glory of God.

Roll Away the Stone of Limitation

The highest teaching of the ages concerns how to pass over from darkness to light, how to roll away the stone of limitation, doubt, and fear, and step forward into an unlimited tomorrow as Divine Love in action.

A well-defined decision carries with it a powerful impact. Without such a decision as to what we really are—a mighty moving Power of Love—and what we want as a result of that understanding, we run the risk of continuing in aimless, perhaps even discordant, pursuits. That would be like jumping up and down and thinking you are going somewhere because you are moving.

Summing up his thoughts on the theory of relativity, Einstein said, "We must make up our mind to accept the fact that the logical basis departs more and more from the facts of experience." Through the study of the Science of Mind, we explore a higher Reality and become one with It; we discover how to think as It thinks.

Ernest Holmes wrote in *Science of Mind* that "we should learn to control our thought processes and bring them into line with Reality." In this way, we allow our choices to be free from anxiety over apparent limitation, confirm our faith in inner Reality and intelligent judgment, and celebrate the experience of the good we decide to accept.

When we roll away the stone of limitation, our Divine Nature unfolds as a stabilizing realization of our oneness with Infinite Life and the recognition of the impartiality and equal availability of all that is wonderful. In this awareness, there is nothing big or little; there are neither important nor unimportant events, conditions, or people.

Peace reigns within the heart of this Reality. We each have an important part in establishing peace on earth as an actuality. We each contribute to the totality of thinking that determines the proceedings of the human experience.

Letting this Truth be our way allows us to view all substance through the eyes of Spirit and perceive the Divine. Generosity, inclusion, and love become our experience, and we honor our responsibility toward peace. Establish this

Truth in your mind, and it rolls away the stone and becomes a living Reality in the experience of all people everywhere. It is the result of following the inspiration of the Spirit within us, which impresses Its certain wisdom upon our hearts.

The decisions we make in life based on this clarity allow us to depart from the tomb of negative thinking and experience and move into the Light of Truth, accomplishing the wonderful as we roll away the stone of limitation.

Develop Acute Perception

Our awareness of our oneness with Infinite Intelligence is restorative, loving, and totally compelling. Our creative minds are ingenious and our lives are masterfully lived when we choose to grow into the consciousness and experience of greater good.

When we search for and find our greater Self and live from our discovery, we become acutely perceptive of the positive. Then the positive becomes acutely perceptive of us.

Ernest Holmes wrote, "What we are looking for, we are looking with." In the *Dhammapeda*, the Buddha taught that "through zeal, knowledge is gained; through lack of zeal, knowledge is lost; let a man who knows this double path of gain and loss thus place himself that knowledge may grow."

A compilation of the wisdom of every age tells us there is a Universal Power that does unto us according to our belief. If we let go and let It lead us into the experience we desire, believing It is doing so, It will. It will because we are already there in Truth.

Acutely perceptive consciousness is free to celebrate newness in life. Such an approach immediately ensures our receptiveness to a healthy mind, body, and world. This allows us to reveal to ourselves, in an astonishingly loving manner, our relationship to the Creative Source of Power and the Law of Mind, in us, as us, and through us.

Tap the Reservoir of Creative Power

Our mind is said to be like an iceberg that floats in the ocean. The tenth of the iceberg we can see above the water line represents our conscious mind. The nine tenths we cannot see can be compared to a deep reservoir of creative power, or the subconscious mind.

Emerson drew his inspiration from what he called the "Over-Soul," the universal repository of all knowledge and power. This is the Divine resource, which is infinite and available to all who are willing to discover it.

With the conscious mind, we choose, judge, and reason. We move through our experience accepting or rejecting what seems good or not so good, or desirable or undesirable as the case may be.

Whatever our mind dwells upon as cause, moves by the Law of Mind and becomes our experience or effect. This teaches us that if we do not like the effect, all we have to do is change the cause; the effect must change as a consequence.

What we are dealing with is the mighty moving Power of Infinite Intelligence. We are made in the image of the Creative Mind of God. As we let the good, the true, and the positive be our way, healthy success begins to dominate our thinking. The result is a happy, poised, and integrated personality and world.

Affirm: *I let the good, the true, and the positive be my way.*

Realize the Spiritual in Everything

Ernest Holmes was fond of saying, "There is nothing more spiritual than a ham sandwich." The Mystic Mind knows that everything everywhere is the Presence of God as form. This is a revelation. Freeing ourselves to think as the Presence thinks, see as It sees, act as It acts, and love as It loves is the "revelation of the revelation." The spiritual Life of all that exists celebrates Itself as us.

With this realization of the spiritual, our theme song becomes, "I have plenty of plenty." We never again feel separated from God, and we evolve into a greater belief in abundance and faith in unlimited possibility. We grasp the greatness of our possibilities and embody the concept that, as Holmes stated so often, *God in us, as us, is us.* It is more than any single individual, or all individuals. It is everything and everyone at once.

The never-ending expansion of our capacity for living greatly and our joy in partaking of the Divine Gift become the loving front edge of our life. We let the Center of Infinite Stability express itself. Health, strength, and security are then reflected into our world, unfold as spiritual understanding, and increase our contributions to all experience.

The key to unlocking this awareness within ourselves can be found by exploring Romans 12:2 even further: "Be ye transformed by the renewing of your mind, and ye may prove what is the good and acceptable and perfect will of God."

God is in everything. There is truly nothing more spiritual than a ham sandwich!

Chapter Eight

The Power of a
Streamlined Consciousness

As the egg must be fertilized to become a bird, so must a command in consciousness (an idea believed in) be fertilized by being emotionalized with acceptance and feeling. This is why it is important to understand what our commands of consciousness really are.

Negative thought and its spoken words produce negative events. Positive thought and its spoken words produce positive events. A command of consciousness will not return to us void. Every idea that passes through our consciousness and our body into the world returns *only* to us—not to anyone else! It does not matter what others might think or say about us, because their word will return to them. The only thing we have to be concerned about is what we ourselves think, believe, and say.

Master Your Command of Consciousness

In the biblical scriptures, there is a statement accredited to the master teacher Jesus that explains that our words are Spirit, and Light, and Truth—and they accomplish what they are sent to accomplish. And our words return to us fulfilled. This is one of the greatest definitions ever given of the command of consciousness unfolding as reality.

The command of consciousness begins as a thought or idea in the mind. There is a metaphysical idea that is as old as time that "thoughts are things." An idea moving through our consciousness becomes experience by way of Law.

A command in consciousness is a thing, just as an egg is a bird that has not yet hatched but has the possibility of becoming a bird. Similarly, an idea has the possibility of becoming a physical fact in our world.

We may remember a time when we had unhappy, depressed, and lonely thoughts and no physical energy. A negative command in consciousness did that. It made us feel as if we weighed a ton. But when we feel upbeat and happy from a positive command, even if we weighed 2,000 pounds, we would feel light as a feather.

Whatever we command in consciousness and fertilize with our emotions and feelings will find a place to emerge. This can happen in an organization, a home, or a relationship. When someone starts expressing fear, soon the whole thing falls apart. Why? Because of the command of consciousness that controls it. It is not always the *intention* that creates what people experience; it is always the *sum total* of the ideas, thoughts, and words that act as a command in consciousness.

Affirm: *My words are Spirit. My words are Light. My words are Truth. They accomplish where they are sent. They return to me fulfilled.*

Expand Your Self-Expression

The world in which we live is alive with the Consciousness of God, which is Infinite Spirit and Divine Energy. Through Law, this Power has become our experience as the visible world in which we live, move, and have our being.

When we worry ourselves into a negative experience, we have matter-of-factly used the Law of the Universe to become the experience through which we are moving. When we change our mind and encourage ourselves in a positive way, the Law of the Universe responds to this inner demand and reestablishes happiness, health, and harmony to our mind, body, and world.

As we let go and let our daily thought and creative expectation unfold from a joy-inspired understanding, infinite supply becomes the positive abundance of our life. The Consciousness of God becomes our experience according to our understanding of it.

In *The Principles of Psychology*, William James captured this idea brilliantly:

We need only in cold blood ACT, as if the thing in question were real, and keep acting as if it were real, and it will infallibly end by growing into such a connection with our life that it will become real. It will become so knit with habit and emotion that our interests in it will be those which characterize belief.

Our daily challenge is to set our goals and identify ourselves with affirmative success in everything we undertake and see ourselves accomplishing all the good we have planned. A wider vision plus a greater sense of self-expression equals abundant living.

Choosing to be a gift of good is an expression of love, good-will, and healthy self-respect to everyone with whom we are involved. No other gift possesses so much potential for greater good, and it provides dividends for ourselves and those we love. It allows us to be open and receptive to greater good, richer opportunities, and Divine guidance as we embrace a fuller concept of our true worth as Divine beings. We are then free to recognize the worth in everyone and dissolve any barriers of separation, competition, or resistance in our consciousness and our world.

Wield Your Force of Perseverance

In the heart and mind of every person, a deep urge propels us toward the experience we call happiness. The words of the Declaration of Independence ordain our right to life, liberty, and the pursuit of happiness. This guarantees the right to *pursue*.

The mystic minds of the ages have taught us pursuit is an inner—not an outer—adventure. Happiness unfolds when we master the art of purposeful living. The eighteenth-century man of letters Samuel Johnson shared that "all the performance of human art, at which we look with praise or wonder, are instances of the resistless force of perseverance."

We become this resistless force in action when we develop an awareness of God in us, as us, and let this awareness evolve into a new philosophy of life. Emerson stated in his speech "Progress of Culture" that "great men are they who see that spiritual is stronger than any material force, that thoughts rule the world."

Happy living hinges upon our capacity to believe successfully in the beautiful. As we harness and master the power of living by constantly drawing upon our inner Source for strength, intelligence, and love, we discover that we are truly unconquered by the world. Being unconquered by limitation, doubt, or fear, we automatically become positive plans of actions, in action. We know what we must do and when and how to do it. We embrace our opportunities and celebrate them because we know we create our own destinies. It is our nature to be creative, and we honor our self-expression by loving our work.

We enhance our self-expression as we balance our work with the joy of our play. This frees us to pause (however briefly), relax into laughter, and return to the demands of the world with renewed vigor. The secret is to move in consciousness from thinking *about* Infinite Life to thinking *as* Infinite Life thinks. By our thought, we exert the Power of Life, if we know the secret.

In his 1946 book *Rediscovery of Christ*, Joseph Lowrey Fendrich wrote:

The development of the idea that man shares in the mind of God is literally true and it is the major teaching of Jesus. For us to go into the Secret Place, as Jesus taught, means simply this—that in the consciousness of man is the mysterious place of power, from which he sends out into his external affairs that influence which brings prosperity, health and success, or from which, on the other hand, he may send out influences that bring returns in failure and unhappiness. *We meet God in our thinking.* By our thoughts we exert the power which is liberty and life, if we know the secret.

The key to a new life is always within us. When we open our doors of awareness, we are filled with the motivation and guidance that allow us to set and accomplish new goals, unleash our hidden potential, and enjoy more and more of life's satisfaction. Thought is creative. History provides us with abundant proof that positive, purposeful thought creates experience—past, present, and future.

Affirm: *I am unconquered by limitation, doubt, or fear. I am a positive plan of action, in action.*

Direct Your Power to Make All Things New

Emerson wrote about the power of rejoicing in our ability to retreat from all torment simply by focusing our thoughts on the Invisible Heart. Not to be merely soothed, but to be replenished; not to be compensated, but to receive the inner power to make all things new.

Self-realization reveals to each of us the mysteries of the kingdom of heaven. As we expand spiritually, we begin to understand the concept that God made us in Its image and likeness and gave to each of us Its unlimited creative power and love. Even in our most unlimited imaginations, we cannot comprehend or encompass all God is, but we are able to embody the idea that all *we* are is God.

The word we speak is the Word of God. The Law of the Infinite is the Law of our being, and this Law responds to and is controlled by the One Power—the Intelligence of Divine Mind. We direct this same unlimited Law and set it in action through what we believe and expect. We never receive more than we expect, and we never keep more than we are ready to be responsible for. An old Irish blessing says, "May you live as long as you want, and never want as long as you live."

The Law of Infinite Love is guided and directed by each of us when we act as if our good is good enough to be true. It is used wisely and confidently when we know the real person we are within, the Self that has all the attributes of Divine Love.

Affirm: *The good I am experiencing is always good enough to be true.*

Psalm 13:6 affirms this in another way: "I will sing unto the Lord, because he hath dealt bountifully with me." With this affirmation in action as the truth of our lives, we unfold as continuous states of well-being rather than as spasmodic acquisitions of health, wealth, or happiness. Positive progress, success, and the capacity for living as love become our daily experiences. We freely celebrate our wise and wonderful use of our supply, discovering that our true wealth is never exhausted; it is felt by every person who is in any way included in the activities of our generously enriched experiences.

We nurture our bountifully supplied lives by a sustained consciousness of an abundance of good. Our evidence of wealth and greater good is but a reflection of the conviction that our provision is adequate, not only for today, but for all the days ahead. We are abundantly prospered.

Affirm: *I celebrate my wise and wonderful use of my supply. My Divine Wealth is never exhausted.*

Recognize What Is Everywhere at Once

Powerful mystic awareness comes to us from the heart and mind of St. Hildegard of Bingen, who summed up the power of God:

> Now here is the image of the power of God: this firmament is an all-encompassing circle. No one can say where this wheel begins or ends. . . . Just as a circle embraces all that is within it, so does the God-head embrace all. No one has the power to divide this circle, to surpass it, or to limit it. God has arranged all things in the world in consideration of everything else.

Enrichment of life depends on embodying the spiritual concept of the all-encompassing circle. We wake up and realize that filling our heads and vocabulary with metaphysical ideas is in itself not going to change our lives for the better. But an acceptance of the Divine within us, our understanding that underneath are the everlasting arms, and our use of knowledge of metaphysical Principle to release our greater good *will* change our lives for the better. This is the Love of God, greeting Itself as our experience. Emerson called it "the opulence of human nature, which can run out to infinitude in any direction." This is Divine opulence in action.

If Infinite Life is a circle that has no circumference, then everything is Its center. God, being everywhere at once, is always right where we are, unfolding forever. The lesson of the all-encompassing circle is that something wonderful is happening now, because something wonderful is always happening everywhere at once.

Unwrap the Gift of God

The Bible tells us, "It is your Father's good pleasure to give you the Kingdom" (Luke 12:32). What is the gift of God, and when is it ours? We are the gift, and it arrived with us, as us, when we arrived in this experience.

The Kingdom is here within us. Heaven is our moment in forever, which is before us now.

How do we open this wonderful gift and embrace it as the wisdom of our way? By dedicating ourselves to our positive purpose, our greater life, and reminding ourselves that wherever our mind goes, our world follows!

Once we have set out upon this course, it becomes easy to behold our positive self-definition with approval and delight. In fact, it becomes a matter of self-preservation, out of which come love, beauty, self-esteem, and spontaneous appreciation for all the other gifts in our experience. This blossoms until we no longer have any reason to criticize anything or anyone.

It is basic to the Principle of our Science that things are the effect of thought, and we are the thinker. The thinker is greater than the thought, and the thought is greater than the thing.

If we think from the truth of our being—as a mighty, moving individualized Power of God in our experience—we are free. We are free to think from the awareness that we are as healthy as the healthiest thought within us. We are the gift of God from Itself, to Itself, now.

Swim against the Stream

Until we are about eight years old, we live in a world of magical thinking. Then we begin to understand cause and effect. But many people find it difficult to let go of the concept of magic, so they keep it alive as superstition. They never quite understand that a winner is a winner because of his or her winning consciousness, and a loser is a loser because of a losing consciousness, no matter where the blame is placed.

Humorist W. C. Fields liked to quip that "a dead fish can float downstream, but it takes a live one to swim upstream." A great mystical truth can be found in Matthew 25:29, where it is written, "For unto every one that hath shall be given, and he shall have abundance; but from him that hath not even that which he hath shall be taken away." This means we can use our imagination to create reasons why we *can*—and swim against the stream—or reasons why we *cannot*, and be content to float along with the status quo.

We cannot be more prosperous and successful until we begin to think as prosperity and success would think, and we cannot do this until we truly love ourselves. Our state of conscious self-definition determines the boundaries within which we desire to live. Self-rejection is the root of all the limitations and ailments of the human experience. Self-esteem and self-assurance know that faith, reason, success, and prosperity are not destinations; they are journeys against the stream of worldly thinking.

Chapter Nine

The Heartbeat of the Infinite

Every person has the ability to become one with the heart-beat of the Infinite and flow with an affirmative attitude. Anyone can have a body, life, and world free from disease and see events unfolding in harmony and successful accomplishment. Lack and limitation in our lives cease to exist as we cease to create and nourish them. They wither away for lack of thought and belief to sustain them.

Make Your Attitude Your Backbone

Teaching people how to live at the level of their highest potential is the most important of all arts. The key to this experience unfolds by way of attitude.

Attitude is the backbone of a positive, spiritual, mental, and physical state of awareness. All thinking people know that an optimistic attitude toward life evolves into vigorous and healthy living. Likewise, a negative, pessimistic, tentative approach to life develops limitation and a habit of blaming bad luck or fate for any misfortune. A worry-free mind views life as refreshing, loving, and challenging, knowing it is a waste of time and energy to worry.

The master teacher Jesus taught us that it is done unto us as we believe. This means that through our belief, we are forever directing the Creative Power to bring joy or unhappiness as our experience. Once we know how important our beliefs are to us, we will be less concerned about the thoughts of others. We are a seed after our own kind. The seed of Life is our consciousness. Our consciousness is our thoughts, ideas, and words. The greatness of each person is a thing we cannot see. It is the Power of God in us, as us. We are each an equal part of the Presence of God within everyone.

We change an appearance only by changing the action that produced it, and we know that every action begins as an idea in mind. Ultimately, our own consciousness must be in accord with Divine perfection if we would experience abundance, harmony, and health. This eternal gift of Life has been proclaimed by the wise, the good, and the great of every age.

"By faith we understand that the worlds have been framed by the word of God, so that what is seen hath not been made out of things which appear" (Hebrews 11:3).

Understand How Life Truly Works

Life works *for* us by working *through* us at the level of our consciousness. We can raise our consciousness by understanding that the dictionary is the only place where *success* comes before *work*.

In his self-reflective book *Meditations in Wall Street*, nineteenth-century stockbroker Henry Stanley Haskins wrote that "the inward light is forever striving to gather enough additional light to penetrate the fog of our senses. What lies behind us and what lies before us are tiny matters compared to what lies within us."

We will not find many rules for success that will work unless *we* do. If at first we do not succeed, we need to find out *why* before we try again. If we are teachable, we will learn how to move from trying to make success happen to becoming one with the law of success and letting it happen. Then we can enthusiastically choose to start a thing and finish it.

An illustration of the "hang in there and keep going for it" philosophy can be found in the story of the man who called the firm of Krupnik, Krupnik, Krupnik, and Krupnik. He asked for Mr. Krupnik. The voice at the receiving end answered, "He is not in."

"All right," said the man, "let me talk to Mr. Krupnik."

"He's not in."

"I'll talk to Mr. Krupnik then."

"He's not here."

"How about Mr. Krupnik?"

"Speaking!"

People who do not find the magic within themselves will always seek it in someone or something else.

This ultimate lesson in truth has been handed down to us by every great teacher of every age. It is the starting place for the formula for success, love, health, and happiness in action. A teacher is not a true teacher if she leads us only to herself. A true teacher teaches in such a way that her students can replace her.

Life also works *for* us by working *through* us at the level of our awareness, by way of our choice. And we cannot live a choiceless life. Our challenge is to choose to be curious about the Truth of our Being.

Curiosity entails a readiness to be enlightened. Raymond Charles Barker believed that intellectual and spiritual curiosity is the only valid excuse for one's existence. A Divine Urge within forever pushes us onward and upward to greater achievement. And we can cooperate with that Divine Urge.

The greatest factor in our lives is our inner attitude about ourselves. Our bodies and world respond to what we think. Our well-being depends on our affirmative thinking and choosing. Our healthy change for the better starts with positive self-identity and a loving understanding of our relationship to the Power that created us out of Itself. This adventure in self-realization brings us to the awareness that we are greater than we think we are. Always.

Our positive, prosperous future depends on the self-expression of our Divine individuality, not conformity to mediocrity. The decisions we make now, and the course we follow as a result, will unfold as our experience, by way of Law. That is how Life works.

Think What (and How) the Great Have Thought

Now it's time to ponder two questions.

First, what is the "I" that everyone uses? The good, the great, and the wise of the ages have referred to it as our individual use of the divine spark, which resides in every person.

Second, can anyone use your "I" for you? Absolutely not! Your use of "I" is your responsibility.

The commandment that we should not take the name of God in vain means we ought never use the phrase "I am . . ." followed with a negative idea. Any time we couple "I" with a thought of doubt or fear, that statement contradicts our highest good. So we should not be surprised if the very thing we doubt or fear appears in our experience.

We are using a principle of thought parallel to the notion in physics that action and reaction are equal to the thoughts themselves. When we become one with the ideas that support our positive welfare rather than oppose it, we may be certain that we will experience the corresponding good. When we become the consciousness of what we want, it appears in our lives.

What the great have thought, we can think. If we are not demonstrating massive good in our lives, it is time to start thinking like those who have. We must develop an inner concept of ourselves that sounds something like this:

Affirm: *I am all qualities necessary to accomplish my desires. I have absolute faith in myself. I have no interest in any suggestion that would tempt me to doubt myself or to be afraid.*

In *Science of Mind*, Ernest Holmes stated: "Such is the power of right thinking that it cancels and erases everything unlike Itself. It answers every question, solves all problems, is the solution to every difficulty."

Affirm: *I place no limit on Principle. I let this Truth be my way!*

Practice Positive Self-Encouragement

The purpose of every part of this book is to teach us how to have healthy, successful, and positive results in our lives, above and beyond conventional belief. In other words, to experience daily what the world calls "miracles."

What is a miracle? It is simply the unfoldment of a natural law that we have not yet raised our consciousness high enough to understand. We are all on an upward journey, and each day reveals new wonders and delights. Every day, we can choose to hone our teachability and obtain an intelligent and substantial spiritual education through study, understanding, and experience.

Appropriately implemented, this way of being frees us to allow great things to happen and teaches us to be responsible for great things when they arrive. Positive reinforcement and healthy rewards develop from correct knowing. Correct inner and outer behaviors come from the One Infinite Source demonstrating Itself as two primary sources: you, and that which teaches you.

The Invisible Power is always available to each of us. Great men and women throughout the ages have known this secret. They called on the Power in time of need and tapped into It for inspiration. Their greatness came through understanding that their intelligence, strength, and positive right action came not from themselves, but from a Power for good beyond any finite capacity to comprehend.

This Power works for Itself, as us, by working through Itself as our choice. As we completely accept our greater good and let unbiased acceptance be our way, the demonstration is made by way of our doing and being.

Our positive progress depends on three factors:

1. Our commitment to a healthy level of positive achievements;

2. Our interest in the art of creative thought in action; and

3. Our purpose in learning it, celebrating it, doing it, and being it.

The amount of quality time we give ourselves for positive self-encouragement always pays off in great and wonderful ways.

The success of Infinite Mind in action, as us, will depend on us and how we obtain our understanding and develop it in wisdom by doing something with it. When Ernest Holmes wrote of our inner light in *Science of Mind*, he summed it up perfectly: "As the inner light dawns, it delivers the outer life from bondage."

Live the Best Time of Your Life

Living in love is the best time of our lives. This occurs when we let go and let the Creative Power in us, as us, move *from* love *through* love *to* love—creating the ever-greater good that is ours by right of consciousness.

We achieve this by aligning with Meister Eckhart's insight that "the eye in which I see God is the same eye in which God sees me." Eckhart also said, "The person who hopes to escape

God . . . cannot escape him. All hiding places reveal God; the person hoping to escape God runs into his lap." Simply put, God is at home. It is we who have gone out for a walk.

The need is great for everyone to celebrate the manifestation of more love, greater creative self-expression, and positive self-understanding. This frees us to become loving assets at home, in business, in the community, and in the world.

The answer to any problem is a love that reaches out from us and enfolds our lives everywhere at once. Ernest Holmes avowed that he had not learned to love well until he learned to love widely. As he put it in *Science of Mind*, "One who has learned to love all people will find plenty of people who will return that love."

The mystic minds of every age have known that love always *includes* and never *excludes*. Living from this Truth allows us to greet all God's offspring—all God's creations—including ourselves.

Accept the Gift of Life

Every day, we have the opportunity to awaken to the Truth of ourselves. When we do, we realize that the mistakes, confusion, and negatives of yesterday are not reality but events we have moved through. That was then; this is now.

We can each be in the now and awaken to view the real life that is ours. Our wonderful dreams are good enough to be true and will become our experience, somehow, somewhere. So why not now?

Life is ours to experience with joy. Life is health of mind, body, and world. Life is prosperity, positive success, and abundant goodness. Life is love. As metaphysicians, we are learning to never expect, accept, or embody less than all of Life.

Success and prosperity in home, work, and play are elements of the gift of Life. We can place our consciousness and experience in the middle of this awareness and Affirm: "It is my good pleasure to receive God's gift now!"

In this way, whatever we need to know in order to let go and let our life succeed is made known to us. We discover how to refuse to place our good merely in the future. Our life becomes a celebration of the prosperous successful activity of Infinite Intelligence in us, as us, now.

Awakening from the dream of world thinking, we find ourselves constantly aware, alert, alive, and magnificently free. As Emerson stated in his 1867 speech at Harvard University, "Power obeys reality, and not appearances; power is according to quality, and not quantity."

Embrace the Promise of Greater Things

The mystic minds of every age have all agreed that there is one Life, that Life is God, and that Life is our life, now.

They have all taught, in their own ways, that when we are one with the truth of ourselves we know and honor the unlimited possibilities of good forever attracting our attention. We can all demonstrate everything we accept as our experience. We can keep everything for which we are willing to be responsible.

God gives to Itself, as us, all that It is. Exploring the best of Self each day will reveal the possibilities within us.

The great English writer H. G. Wells said: "All this world is heavy with the promise of greater things, and a day will come, one day in the unending succession of days, when beings, beings who are now latent in our thoughts and hidden in our loins, shall stand upon this earth as one stands upon a footstool, and shall laugh, and reach out their hands amid the stars."

This promise stimulates us to live a larger life and experience freedom from everything that could limit us. Every day is our opportunity to give birth to the great and wonderful as our life, to expand spiritually and reach out our hands amid the stars. And so we become like Raymond Charles Barker, who firmly believed that the only power he had was God, and *that*, he felt, was sufficient to revolutionize his being.

Affirm: *I am willing to be a good steward of my every thought, word, and action. I demonstrate this willingness with everything and everyone in my life today.*

Chapter Ten

The Power of Planning
Your Positive Purpose

To build a bridge or a skyscraper, an architect must first have a blueprint and a plan of the structure he or she has decided to create. In fashioning and directing our unfoldment of life, we must first have a design and pattern for the power of our intelligence to follow.

When the blueprint of our experience is clear and celebrating itself within us, we can apply the correct technique for moving from thought to thing, and our completed expression corresponds with our state of consciousness. We joyously find ourselves in tune with the Universe, surrendering ourselves completely to the healing power of greater good. We know the Power that creates and supports everything is healing, building, and sustaining our world for the better.

Master Your Operating Manual

The great teachings of every age have passed to us the understanding that as we accept the Allness of Infinite Intelligence as the basis for our lives, we will prosper in every phase of it. Knowing that Divine Mind is living our lives and manifesting perfection frees us to understand that the same Power that demonstrates our positive opportunities also guides us in making the most of them.

There is a correct technique for operating everything: television, DVD player, automobile, computer, and (more importantly) our thoughts. Longtime Religious Science minister Robert Scott used to tell me, "You are free to be what you choose to be in thought, feeling, and attitude; the transformation takes place deep within your consciousness and then is outwardly confirmed in your world of experience."

In this way, we are no longer subject to the world's beliefs about age, opportunity, ability, prosperity, health, or happiness. We know that fear and failure do not belong to us because we recognize that we are one with the Infinite, which is active within us, as us.

When we become one with the correct technique for greater living, we are resurrected from any and all self-imposed limitation. We rise above all unpleasant conditions, feelings of inferiority, belief in disease, and sense of loneliness. Why? Because we are spiritual beings, inhabiting human bodies and flowing through the perfect, friendly Universe God created out of Itself. We are triumphant, joyous, wise, and free when we choose to be born anew in our hearts, souls, and minds, every moment of every day.

We can choose to rise above every challenge and lay a claim upon our own attention. When we attune to the Love of God, it enables us to close our thinking to any negative suggestion the world has to offer. Power within us, as us, depends only upon our recognition of it.

Embody Your Infinite Potential

As we discover the wisdom of the great thinkers who inspired Ernest Holmes and other New Thought leaders, we begin to see clearly the Golden Thread that binds them all together. That Golden Thread is the awareness that Infinite Potential lies within each and every person, and It gives to Itself, as us, according to the manner in which It is used.

If we want to let go and let our lives become as beautiful as they can be, we must work with Infinite Potential in our heart, mind, and consciousness—in the way Infinite Potential works. We must free ourselves from negative thinking and limited ideas about ourselves and others, cut ourselves free from old hurt and pain through forgiveness, and give positive self-direction and love to our world.

Each of us has the freedom to choose and to cultivate the cause of healthy greatness. Whether or not we do this is of no concern of Infinite Potential. It neither knows nor cares that in one place It is used in a loving, healthy, and intelligent way, and abused in another. God is the Infinite Potential of all experience. As it is written in Ephesians 4:6, there is "one God and Father of all, who is over all, and through all, and in all."

The glory of life is that it responds by corresponding. This glory is within each of us, as us, ever awaiting our recognition of it. We each deserve to have good and greater good flourishing and growing in our life in wonderful ways.

Every ending is a new beginning, and every new day can be a new beginning for a new faith. This clear realization removes all nonsense and doubt from us, for we know the eternal is the Truth of our being, and it heals every circumstance that needs to heal as we learn to celebrate the Infinite Potential of Life.

Let us evolve our faith in God into the faith *of* God by becoming one with the Golden Thread of Truth. Know that Infinite Potential is the advancing edge of our way.

Perfect the Art of Self-Persuasion

Those who enjoy the greatest share of life's rewards are often those who have learned the art of positive self-persuasion. Each of us can develop this art if we are willing to study and practice certain principles and put them to use in our daily lives.

To live successfully, we must be sold on our highest ideas and ideals. To accomplish this, we must be sold on ourselves.

Our challenge is to make a special agreement with ourselves to embody the highest and best of our true nature and live our lives from this embodiment. As we do this, we automatically replace failure with success, anxiety with confidence, and fear with courage.

This happens when we replace the seeming logic of dualism—which is based on the concept of opposing principles—with the logic of polarity, which is based on oneness.

Oneness is the central concept of the Mystic Mind. This expanded consciousness spoke through the Buddha, who stated, "Worship not me; the Buddha is within you."

We champion the excellence of Divine Mind in our lives, as our lives, when we practice the art of positive self-persuasion. This is a commitment that must express itself through our hearts and minds as health, happiness, and wholeness.

Affirm: *I now embody the highest and best of my true nature. I live my life from this embodiment. Success, confidence, and courage are my Truth.*

Our thoughts and actions must express themselves as intelligent joy, manifested in the never-ending now. Any feelings of inadequacy vanish as we let go and know we deserve to be happy, healthy, and fulfilled. Ernest Holmes taught that our belief and conviction about the Reality that exists behind all things should be emotionally acceptable, intellectually sound, and, above all, practical and demonstrable in our lives.

We can tell we are on the right course when we can observe our "self-advocating" excellence everywhere in our experience. We know in our hearts that the Universe supports Itself, as us. Positive direction becomes our normal path, and perfect unfoldment fills our every experience. Our challenge is to let the gently flowing stream of Infinite Love bless our lives and all the lives we touch. We need to discipline our minds to thoughtful and intelligent spiritual attitudes toward our world and everyone in it.

It is easy to set in motion an affirmative pattern of peace, harmony, love, joy, and success in all circumstances. We can be appreciative of every day, knowing in Truth that we are kind, considerate, and capable of being the best we can be, right now. When we celebrate God's excellent results, only joy can remain in consciousness.

In his book *Spirit and Reality*, the Russian philosopher Nikolai Berdyaev wrote, "Spirit is the reality revealed in and through the existential subject, a reality emanating from within rather than from without, from the objective world." The Psalmist stated, "The Lord is my shepherd; I shall not want" (Psalms 23:1). And Carl Jung quoted an utterance of the Delphic oracle that said, "Called on or not, God will be present."

As we assimilate and enjoy greater awareness and practice self-persuasion, we demonstrate greater well-being.

"Good Enough" Never Is

Living by our understanding of Principle crumbles all former barriers. We become revitalized positive faith in action, and the way of our heart becomes the heart of our way. Our world and everyone in it responds with joyous expectancy.

When our thoughts are filled with comfortable nonsense, stress, doubt, and fear accumulate in us and cause negation in our lives, and we start to feel like a debris-clogged river. Get rid of the obstruction, and the water gushes in a positive flow and a surge of power. This same thing happens within us when we let go and realize the only thing impeding the progress of our greater good is our thought, not the substance and effect of people or events.

In order to master where we want to be, we must master where we are and give our very best to it. Love unfolds us into harmony with the greatness we are in Truth. Being God in action demands a zest for life, as well as a stimulating interest in our choices, our world, the people around us, and our aspirations and dreams as well as those of our neighbors and loved ones.

Good enough is never good enough when we unleash our greatness. We do this by turning in thought to the Divine Center of Strength within us. We realize our oneness with Infinite Greatness. We know that out of the One Life, we are fully supplied and renewed in body, mind, and spirit.

Being a well-adjusted part of God, we delight in the progress of never-ending self-awareness. We are never alone when we love greatly. Divine Greatness as Love is the most powerful incentive we can ever be, do, experience, and know. Without our awareness of Spirit's expression through us, we are not wholly alive, awake, or great.

When we think as Divine Greatness thinks, our love includes our Self and our wholehearted acceptance of it. Good enough is never good enough when greatness is our way.

Embrace Your Happy New You

All your dreams are waiting for *you* to come true! How do we "come true" and let our highest goals, desires, and dreams be our way? There is a great lesson concerning this very question contained within the powerful affirmation, "I am the voice of God explaining Itself to Itself by means of me."

We are all greater than we think we are. To be new in the now, we must wake up to a new understanding of the majesty of our being and be new within that discovery. It is important to recognize this, because there is a desire inherent in each of us to reveal and express our majesty. Even so, many people still operate at a level of understanding and consciousness far removed from the Truth of themselves.

The Principle we practice as Religious Scientists is the same one followed by every great and wise person who ever lived. As happy, healthy, and successful people allow their excellence to manifest through their talent, creativity, career, and loving relationships, they discover at a deeper level that they are not *getting* something but *giving* something. These people give authentically, from the Truth of themselves.

When we know (knowing there is always more to know), our new knowing, once applied, becomes new wisdom and unfolds as our new now! In his essay "Experience," Emerson wrote, "Into every intelligence there is a door which is never closed, through which the creator passes." Choose to be one with a consciousness that affirms new awareness.

Minnie Louise Haskins' 1908 poem "God Knows" is most familiar under the title "The Gate of the Year." It was quoted by King George VI of England during his 1939 Christmas broadcast:

And I said to the man who stood at the gate of the year:
"Give me a light that I may tread safely into the unknown."
And he replied:
"Go out into the darkness and put your hand into the hand
*   of God.*
That shall be to you better than light and safer than a
*   known way."*

The lesson for us is to begin, this moment, to unfold into our new now with faith and trust in the Intelligence that dwells within us and thinks and acts through us, as us.

There is a growing need for a faith unencumbered by dogma and orthodoxy. A new now is the outgrowth of freedom of outlook from the Truth of our being. It is about deeper insight, permitting our fuller expression of Spirit. This is the path of positive growth, advancement of greater good, and stress-free self-expression.

These are the conclusions drawn by Dr. Ernest Holmes, the founder of our teaching—and the findings of many other brilliant minds of his day and ours. Let their wisdom be your way.

Be in the Now

In the mind and heart of every human being reside the age-old questions:

"Who and what am I?"

"What is my purpose?"

"What is my potential?"

Each of us can find our own satisfactory answers to these questions from the writings of the great thinkers and teachers, from the clear impartation of Universal Principle, and from our inner selves. Once these are found and embodied, purposeless living disappears from our experience.

The great Intelligence that created the Universe and everything in it out of Itself is lovingly experiencing Itself as us—one life at a time, one day at a time, and one moment at a time. This is why the great have told us to be in the now.

When we understand and celebrate what we know we are, we see our yesterday through our *now* awareness instead of trying to see our now through *yesterday's* awareness. We develop our inner ability to bear up under the knowledge of the wonders and unlimited potential of our life. We realize that, by way of the Highest Power of Mind, the greater dimension we shall one day express as our life will fulfill itself in our world as soon as we are responsible for the dimension we are in now.

Think Strong to Live Strong

One of the many ways the Science of Mind teaching benefits its students is through their discovery—within themselves— of the illumination needed to brighten the dark corners where fear, despair, lack, and ill-health lurk. This Infinite Loving Power is available to everyone, everywhere, through positive prayer, or what we call Spiritual Mind Treatment.

In his essay "The American Scholar," Emerson wrote: "Character is higher than intellect. Thinking is the function. Living is the functionary. The stream retreats to its source. A great soul will be strong to live, as well as strong to think."

This Power is unfailing. It does not depend on anything outside Itself, because there *is* no outside. It depends only on our use of It and our faith in the effectiveness and infallibility of Divine Mind. It is applicable to every problem, big or little, in every part of our lives.

If we allow the world and our experience to fool us into believing that problems are unsolvable, frustrations appear and divert our thoughts back to the same old negative, wearisome paths that lead nowhere except through a maze of monotonous confusion. To enjoy strong living and strong thinking is to set in motion the Divine fusion that manifests Infinite Light and dispels darkness. In this state of consciousness, we are ready to receive wisdom. As Ernest Holmes stated in *Science of Mind*, "The answer to every question is within [us], because [we are] within Spirit, and Spirit is an Indivisible Whole."

Chapter Eleven

The Power of Unfolding Your Timeless Truth

The captain of a sailboat can sail wherever he desires because it is his servant. Mastery of the power of the wind is possible through the conscious use of intelligence and the ability to become one with the proper conditions.

In the same manner, the Law of Mind within us unfolds from the ideas about ourselves and our world, which are contained within our conscious minds. Wherever we direct our minds, our lives follow.

Seize Your Great Destiny

Out of the hearts and minds of clear, positive thinkers grows the ability to seize a thriving destiny of greater good, a destiny of being in the moment. Universalist preacher Edwin Hubbell Chapin said that "if you should take the human heart and listen to it, it would be like listening to a seashell; you would hear in it the hollow murmur of the infinite ocean to which it belongs, from which it draws its profoundest inspiration, and for which it yearns."

We seize our destiny of greater good as we flow with the wisdom of Psalm 118:24, which tells us, "This is the day which the Lord hath made; we will rejoice and be glad in it." This allows us to let go, let Infinite Intelligence live Itself through us, and celebrate each hour of every day as an unlimited opportunity we accept with joy.

As we think from this awareness, we discover we are victorious, even in the face of the nonsense of world thinking and its effects. Any perceived difficulties are healed, and we find ourselves calm and free of fear. Our hearts and minds are liberated as we let wisdom fulfill our positive self-appointed actions.

We have the freedom to seize our destinies by choosing what kind of lives we want to live and how we want to live them. We are each a special, unique creation in the Mind of God, and we each can be self-aware, self-choosing, spontaneous, and free.

British physician and preacher Thomas Fuller wrote three books of wisdom for his son. The third was *Gnomologia* (1732), in which he shared the wisdom that a man "does not believe who does not live according to his belief." Our beliefs about ourselves are the blueprint that Infinite Life follows as It becomes our experience.

Our consciousness of life is what we know about life. Nothing exists outside of consciousness. If we feel ourselves to be separated from a positive, prosperous destiny, for all practical purposes, we are. However, when we seize the Truth of ourselves and let Truth in us, as us, seize our destinies, any sense of separation has no reality. We are one with never-ending greater good, free from yesterday and new in the now.

Master the Law of Creative Power

Some people may not be aware of the connection between their experience and their belief. What we feel and believe about ourselves, our situation, and everything in it, has an interesting resemblance to what we experience. The event or experience is objective, while the belief is subjective. Events are visible, and beliefs are invisible.

Many people believe that what happens in their daily world of activity is the result of chance or luck. This, of course, is erroneous thinking. The Universe is always functioning by way of the law of our own belief, and subsequent living only proves the infallibility of this law.

Here is an excellent way to experiment with conscious-ness, prove our positive faith, and direct our experience. First, we can change a deeply held belief about an important aspect of our life, such as success, health, or relationships, then observe (and celebrate) the resulting changes in effect. Second, we can exchange our concept and belief about a person in our life and see what happens. Third, we can watch what we *do*. Why? Because we always do what we believe. We always act according to our faith in ourselves and our world, even though we may articulate something different. Watch what you say and do! This is the clue to your real beliefs.

A person who feels and believes he is inferior, or who thinks the world is unfriendly and difficult, has an underde-veloped capacity for living and loving. He is choosing to deny and inhibit his Divine Urge to express life in a full and successful way. He is sold on the idea that it is safer and easier to do nothing and just let today be a copy of yesterday.

It is a wise and intelligent person who asks herself, "What do I really believe about myself and my world?"

Jesus is quoted as declaring that "all things are possible to him that believeth" (Mark 9:23). This statement is an expression of the Law of Infinite Principle in action. It is the Truth of Being for each and every one of us as we express the creative process of Divine Life according to our belief and faith.

Since our lives are either changing for the positive or the negative, it is wise to know that whenever we choose, we can have anything change exclusively for the better. Let us take the "all things are possible" lesson seriously. Start by believing in your own greatness, and have faith in the Law of Creative Power in a positive and purposeful way.

Claim Your Never-Ending Opportunity

We have the never-ending opportunity to set in motion anything we want and expect. The Universe will give anything at any time *if* we surrender to a positive purpose *and* to our perfection. We can demonstrate anything we desire if we are willing to give one hundred percent to the idea and let God take care of the details. But we must also understand that people will not give what they think they cannot receive.

Are we really ready to commit ourselves to what we say we want? There is a wonderful cosmic Law in the Universe that says, "You do not have to tell me what you want; just give it, and I will give it back to you multiplied." For example, if we want more wonderful people in our lives, we simply allow ourselves to be more wonderful.

If we do not see our way clear in our relationship with any person, place, or thing, the Law of Infinite Mind, as our being, will give us a way out of that relationship. The Universe is perfect. We always get what we really expect, no matter what we say to the world around us. Our challenge is to fill our minds and hearts with enthusiastic anticipation, knowing the Law of Mind in action weaves the pattern of our thought into and as our experience.

Infinite Power must be *recognized* in a greater way before it can be *used* in a greater way. The most important question we can ask ourselves is always, "What do I identify with?" Our challenge is to identify with the Truth of our being, which Ernest Holmes maintained is the objectification of God in human form, the Sonship of the Father.

When we open our hearts, minds, and understanding to the art, history, philosophy, and metaphysical awareness of the past, we enhance our present in a positive way. How do we do this? Emerson, in his essay "Spiritual Laws," hands us this torch of great truth to light our way:

> Real action is in silent moments. The epochs of our life are not in the visible facts of our choice of a calling, our marriage, our acquisition of an office, and the like, but in a silent thought by the wayside as we walk; in a thought which revises our entire manner of life and says, "Thus hast thou done, but it were better thus." This revisal or correction is a constant force, which as a tendency reaches throughout our lifetime.

As we align ourselves with all the love, wisdom, and power in the Universe, we can joyously claim our wonderful heritage. All limitation ends as we "unlimit" our identification with our Creator and let it be steadfast and clear.

Draw Life on a Broader Canvas

Moving forward with our quest, we find the Source of our real selves within us. The mystic minds of the ages have all told us that the possibility of infinite growth and achievement is always within our spiritual grasp, awaiting only our awakening to the Presence, coming forth in all Its magnificence. Einstein is thought to have advised that a man should look for what is, and not for what he thinks should be. Ernest Holmes wrote, "To be real and free, individuality must be created in the image of Perfection and let alone to make the great discovery for itself."

The archetype of infinite excellence, after which the singularity of each of us has been, is, and will always be fashioned, is the Divine archetype. As we set about being the best we know how to be, we move forward on the journey of discovery of the Self. We realize that our individuality is Infinite Life's gift to Itself, and it cannot be disavowed or negated.

If we are having any kind of limited experience, we need to know there is a broader canvas here. This idea allows us to create a greater inner picture and know that our real Self is in full command of our lives. Indestructible Perfection is then free to fill our words, our deeds, our health, and our world.

Affirm: *The Infinite Intelligence that is my real Self is in full command of my life.*

Enter the Field of Prosperous Possibility

Each of us is always at the threshold of a world of richness beyond our fondest dreams. This world of experience contains all the treasures we can think of—and more.

The world we live in, by way of its spiritual Truth, is our treasure chest. All we need, and even greater things, are available to us. It is all ours for the understanding.

We move through the entrance of our prosperous possibility by choosing to commit ourselves to being useful. All treasure houses offer hospitality to a loving and useful mind. This is because a clear, positive mind knows that to achieve healthy success, we need to have a clearly defined purpose. We need the inner and outer things necessary to carry out that purpose, and the correct adjustment of our successful means to our successful ends.

Every human being on planet earth is desirous of something, be it food, spiritual growth, material abundance, recognition, praise, or a helping hand. There are needs to be met everywhere, and the Power of the Infinite Life that created us out of Itself knows what to do and how to do it. Ernest Holmes maintained that the person who is the greatest success is one who fills the most needs. The one who profits most is the one who serves best.

Our challenge is never to be like the person who sits shivering in front of the hearth of life, saying, "Give me heat, and I will give you wood." It does not work that way. What we give, we receive.

Express the Fullness of Truth

Nothing gives a greater feeling of satisfaction than to end the day knowing it has been a good one. This deep feeling of quiet happiness engenders our awareness of the promise of a better tomorrow, a divine promise from God—to Itself, as us.

At the end of a good day, let us sit down in a quiet moment and contemplate our experience. What was its quality? Have we missed an opportunity to do a kindness? Have we remembered that a thankful heart is a magnet for good? Did we free our irresistible force? Did we honor our ability to see things in a clear way?

English satirist Joseph Addison wrote in his essay "Discretion" that "a man with great talents, but void of discretion, is like Polyphemus in the fable, strong and blind, endued with an irresistible force, which for want of sight is of no use to him."

While we abide as Life in action, opportunity for greater good will abide at the heart of our experience. This everlasting reality frees us to know that as long as we live, move, and have our being, opportunities of every kind will manifest in our lives. We will also know we deserve to embrace them as they appear, doing the very best we can in thought, word and deed in each moment. The flow of opportunity, health and wholeness is without end. As we sing in an updated version of Clara H. Scott's old hymn "Open My Eyes, That I May See": "My eyes are open. Now I see! Fullness of truth. Illumining me!"

Chapter Twelve

Reveal Your Positive Purpose

Each of us, as a unique, individual, important idea in the mind of God, is the causal, creative, shaping influence of our experience. Our thoughts, choices, and attitudes create the atmosphere in which we live. They lead us to our positive purpose.

Accept the Gift of Self-Leadership

A good leader cares deeply about those he or she is leading. This is especially true in the most important experience of our life: self-leadership. We open the gift of positive self-leadership when we discover that love is unconquerable *and* we learn to let love be our way. This leads to freedom. Freedom already exists, but in an abstract and formless state. It can only take the form our thought gives it.

Depression happens when we get in the way of our own recovery process through a lack of positive self-leadership. What most people define as suffering is really the recovery process, moving forward from grief, hurt, loss, or pain.

We can move away from our sense of bloated nothingness and lead ourselves—as happy, healthy consciousness in action—to a life above and beyond anything we have ever known before. Philosopher Jean-Jacques Rousseau wrote that most people are, in effect, deaf to that internal voice, which nevertheless calls to them so loud and emphatically. A mere machine is incapable of thinking, but in man there exists something perpetually prone to expand and burst the chains by which it is confined.

We can each accept our great gift of positive self-leadership because we are of the quality of Divine Mind. We all have the ability to understand our own true selves, to know who we are and to have a comfortable, healthy, and creative life. We can all recognize our own true nature, and we can have a secure and pleasant life without waiting on circumstances.

To become one with the gift of positive self-leadership and its affirmative embodiment requires us to turn within to the contemplation of the true, the enduring, and the good. This is the meaning of the statement attributed to the master teacher Jesus when he said we should seek the kingdom of heaven first, and all other things would be added unto us.

Every new day offers unlimited opportunities to all of us: setting in motion healthy outlooks and attitudes create an affirmative example for those around us. Every moment gives us an opportunity to advance the spirit of positive self-leadership. As a result of our choices, we can follow our star of greatness. Then the world becomes the fulfillment of peace on earth and goodwill in action.

Follow the Golden Thread

The Golden Thread binds the awareness of the great, the good, and the wise. It encompasses women and men from every class of society and every race. There are spiritual leaders such as Mohammed, Moses, and Jesus; philosophers such as Plato, Emerson, and Thomas Troward; poets such as the Brownings, Whitman, and Shakespeare; scientists such as Curie, Einstein, and Pasteur; and clear, intelligent-thinking people everywhere. The common denominator among all these individuals is the understanding of the ingredients of success and how to apply them—the consciousness of, "It is done unto you as you believe."

Our challenge is to be consciously aware that our real Self is in total command of our livingness, to let go and let the Golden Thread of Truth influence our thoughts, words, and deeds, so we become uplifted in every aspect of our beings. This is positive self-knowing and healthy self-direction in action. The reward is increased wisdom, greater harmony, and a greater degree of beautiful life experience.

All of us can increase our use of Creative Power in stewardship of our positive purpose, no matter how much or how little of our Creative Power is being used in any moment. Every person has a strong inner compulsion, the Divine Urge, not only to heal and demonstrate greater personal good, but also to make a worthwhile contribution to the wonderful world in which we live.

We all remember the story about Aladdin and his magic lamp from *One Thousand and One Nights (Arabian Nights)*. The lamp would work for anyone who possessed it and knew how to use it. The lamp could not say no.

Our Aladdin's lamp is the Divine Creative Power within us, as us, that cannot say no to anything we believe. However, many people fear the responsibility of this priceless possession and thereby limit their achievement in the world.

The wisdom of the Golden Thread tells us that we can discover a new creative high, live more intelligently and more lovingly, and give something that will make life happier and more glorious *right now*.

In *Freedom: Its Meaning*, Einstein touched on the freedom bestowed upon us with this wisdom (when we adhere to it):

Those instrumental goods which should serve to maintain the life and health of all human beings should be produced by the least possible labor of all.... Man should not have to work for the achievement of the necessities of life to such an extent that he has neither time nor strength for personal activities. Without this second kind of outward liberty, freedom of expression is useless for him.

The Roman emperor and philosopher Marcus Aurelius taught us that "men exist for the sake of one another. Teach them then or bear with them."

The possibility of successful achievement and abundant positive growth lies within us, waiting only for our discovery of the Power and Presence to come forth in all Its greatness.

Let us each give thanks for our divine heritage and the privilege of expressing the best of ourselves.

Affirm: *My real self is in total command of my life! I let go and let the Golden Thread of Truth influence my thoughts, words, and deeds.*

Make Your Dreams Come True

No one ever needs to fear the future because everyone is a self-contained source of unlimited good—always accessible and forever exhaustless. The Truth of life's journey is the completeness of Love unfolding. Our awareness and belief in this Truth corrects the undesirable situations in our mind, body, and world.

In the consciousness of every person is the wonderful place of power the Bible calls "the secret place of the Most High" (Psalm 91:1). From this center, we direct each external event that demonstrates success, health, and prosperity. On the other hand, we may influence our world in such a way that the return is unhappiness and failure.

We meet Infinite Life in our thinking. The challenge is to also greet Infinite Life as our thought. If we understand the Principle, active participation in the Divine Potentiality becomes our way.

Theological writer Hosea Ballou believed that a godly life is the strongest argument you can offer the skeptic: "Preaching is to much avail, but practice is far more effective. No reproof or denunciation is so potent as the silent influence of a good example."

The language of our mind is read upon every page of our life. The silent wordlessness of our heart expresses as feeling, motion, and look. It evolves as a life that is truly a song worth singing.

How many of us dream about things we would like to do? Dream about goals we would like to fulfill? Dream about great good we would like to demonstrate in our own life? Then we sit down and dismiss our dreams with questions such as "Why do I deserve that?" The greatest teachers who ever lived taught us that we can achieve anything we can conceive *if* we believe in the concept and know it is already *us*. This is allowing ourselves to have faith in unlimited good in action, as us.

We are each our own unlimited possibility, and there are no restrictions placed on us by anything or anyone, *except ourselves*. We rise above and beyond and let ourselves flow forward as the unlimited experience of self in an unlimited world. We can allow ourselves to discover a higher level of awareness in order to grow to the point where we want to be in life.

If we have a restriction in our life, it is only as permanent as we make it. It is also as temporary as we make it. All God's Power is available to us. Let your light so shine.

Discover Your Positive Direction

Spiritual lessons live wherever men and women seek the Truth that sets us free. Now we examine what this Truth is, and how we can apply it to our lives to discover positive direction and harmony by way of healing confusion and strife.

Living in the Truth that sets us free demands that our lives express our innermost being. The experiential wonder of freedom—as health, abundance, and happiness—demands a conviction and faith that Truth is manifesting now, and that there is a perfect unfoldment of the Power of Divine Life within the individual. Within me. And within you. Within anyone, in any situation.

Ernest Holmes taught that "the armor of God is faith in the good, the enduring and the true. Against such, there is no law. That is, against Truth, nothing can stand. The armor of God suggests protection to those who believe in and trust the law of Good."

We are each an idea in the Mind of God, and God knows how to support Its ideas. If there is any area of our life where we do not think we can improve, we have probably stopped growing in that area.

Understanding this lesson is freedom. Understanding this is knowing that Infinite Mind is the best, and It will never want less for Its creation. It created us out of Itself; therefore, we are the best.

Affirm: *The Truth is manifesting in every corner of my life right now. There is a perfect unfoldment of the Power of Divine Life within this situation.*

Recognize Your Divine Attributes

We all have the capacity to use intelligently the power for good that we are. We can be as happy or as unhappy as we choose to be. According to a Japanese Buddhist meditation, the jewel of the perfect nature, clear and luminous as the sun, dwells in every being.

The ancients recognized that Infinite Life dwells in wholeness, in and as the human being. We are It, and It is us.

To think of ourselves as being only persons—intellect and flesh walking around—is not to have caught God's concept of us as aspects of Itself. God called us out of Itself in order that It might manifest through us as the great masterpieces we are.

We are always one with God. Being of the Infinite, we are also infinite. Sri Ramakrishna taught that the one who finds not the Eternal in himself will never find It outside; but one who sees It in the temple of his own soul, sees It also in the temple of the Universe.

We are equipped with everything we need so that we may know God. Being one with the Infinite, we are entitled to know the Truth of our being—to realize all that belongs to Divine Love also belongs to us.

It is the Father's good pleasure to give you the kingdom. This is the kingdom of fulfillment in which we recognize our divine attributes. As the Bhagavad Gita tells us: "I am the self, established in the hearts of all beings."

Guide the Universe's Response by Your Attitudes

The things we have in life, evaluated the right way and treated astutely, serve us well. The desire for outer wealth and personal advancement is the result of and in keeping with the inner Divine Urge to express.

However, unless we evolve in understanding, we are in danger of becoming owned by an insatiable drive rather than flowing lovingly into stress-free, gratifying accomplishment. Proverbs 2:2 tells us to "incline thine ear unto wisdom, and apply thy heart to understanding."

When we stop squandering our efforts by competing with others, we free ourselves into self-awareness. Did you ever notice how tired you can get when you are doing something you do not want to do? And how much energy and vitality you can feel when you are doing something you love to do? Life works better with inspiring spiritual and mental motivation.

Our rewards are indeed wonderful when we apply this practice to the vast, invisible realm of cause and creativity. When we express our gratitude for health, prosperity, beauty, harmony, love, and joy, we praise our Creator.

We increase the flow of good into our lives when we glorify the Source from which it comes. Ernest Holmes agreed with the world's greatest thinkers when he taught that through an inherent Law of Mind, we increase whatever we praise. You magnify your blessings by knowing the Universe responds generously to your attitude.

Chapter Thirteen

Fine-Tune Your Positive Purpose with Treatment

The Presence:
He comes in beauty and he comes in storm,
But in them both the Presence is revealed
To him who is attuned, and he
Who loves will hear the voice of love.
It is through love that God reveals Himself,
But each attracts from Nature only that
To which he is in pitch, as one harp string
Will echo to another harp in tune
With that same key.

The Farer:
I would to Him be harp
Or string that I may be His instrument
And let the key be love.
—Ernest Holmes and Fenwicke Holmes, *The Voice Celestial*

When we truly love and hear the voice of love, we are in a state of "letting go and letting God" in every aspect of our lives. Love lets all dreams come true, because it is through love that God reveals Itself—from Itself, through Itself, to Itself. Emerson's idea that if one wants a friend, one must be a friend, has been proved often enough to be accepted as truth.

We can take this truth to a higher level by saying that if one wants to be loved, one must be love in action. Being love in action means being loving in thought, word, and deed, and having constant and consistent expectation of greater good.

Become Love Unfolding

An early New Thought teacher, Alberta Smith, shared a powerful description of love unfolding in *I Lift My Lamp*:

> When we come to understand that evil is but a negation, like darkness, having no real substance or place; that God is all there is, this knowledge will enable us to see, once and for all, that evil is a delusion, without power or presence, and it is as silly to spend our time in fighting it, as it would be to waste our strength in combating a shadow. Then we shall be able to adopt the Christ method of nonresistance to evil, and "turn upon it the light of pure goodness and keep it there persistently until the darkness is converted into light" as Ernest Holmes said in *Science of Mind*.

Similarly, we may want to learn how to swim but be terribly afraid of water. We long to conquer this handicap. If we use

Spiritual Mind Treatment to overcome fear by realizing there is nothing to overcome, we then yield to the water and soon can swim and dive in perfect confidence.

In Isaiah 30:15 we are told, "In quietness and in confidence shall be your strength." However, we cannot reach a higher level of positive faith and love without being grateful for what we already have. We must clearly decide what we really want in life and how we want it, and *then* expect it to happen in a stress-free way.

Recently, one of my students shared with me the wonderful results that have followed his commitment to and study of the principles we teach in Science of Mind. When a friend first gave him a copy of the book *A New Design for Living* by Ernest Holmes and Willis Kinnear, my student had been drinking to excess and getting into trouble for a period of years. He began to attend a Religious Science church and enrolled in the Science of Mind classes. He did not just sit and listen; he applied what he heard.

Today, his self-esteem is alive, awake, and well. He has a very good job and loving, vital relationships with his wife and children. He has just bought a new home. Best of all, he has stopped drinking, and his entire disposition has changed so radically that he is living a completely different life than in the previous ten years.

He stated, "I can never express all the gratitude my family and I feel for the blessings of this teaching."

This is but one example of someone who has learned how to turn himself over completely to the Higher Power of Infinite Love, and knows how to feel and celebrate the joy of it.

Start Your Day with Purpose

One cannot live in any community long without realizing how many people spend a great deal of their time in arguments about what they can or cannot accomplish. Instead of flowing forward as love unfolding into a rich, fulfilled life, they undermine themselves with curious illusions about their limitations and reasons why their lives are the way they are and why they must stay in them. People laboring under this self-inflicted handicap can put the brakes on this ordeal by discovering and knowing that at the extremity of their deficiencies, there is always the strength, wisdom, and power of Intelligent Love.

When you start your day, set your goals, contemplate your purpose for achieving them, and let your purpose be the advancing front edge of your decisions. Be the best you know how to be. When you end the day, review and celebrate your accomplishments, sleep worry-free, and wake up enthusiastic about creating another fulfilling day.

The world needs all of us; otherwise, we would not be here. We are all part of the whole and necessary to the betterment of the whole.

Infinite Love made each of us out of Itself as a one-of-a-kind, never-happened-before masterpiece. We are each unique ideals in the Mind of God, moving through our lives and discovering our unlimited potential, so God can discover and experience Itself.

Our challenge is to live, think, and work in the conviction that we are not only wanted but needed. As we let this great truth be our constant inspiration, we find ourselves in a state of freedom beyond anything we may have known. The better we play our part, choosing to be nothing less than all we can possibly be, the greater good grows as the well-being of the whole.

We are here for a purpose: life is too important for us to be created without any reason. Whatever comes and goes, our purpose is to be true to love.

Our thought process should unfold this way: love much, do much, and never do anything that will not add to the happiness and well-being of everyone in our lives.

As love unfolding, our aim should be to reach the heights of possibility so we can delight in the splendor and be examples for others to find the same experience.

As we rejoice in our present blessings and see them through the eyes of love, they are all enhanced and increased. Just as thousands of seeds will be harvested from one seed planted, and a million more harvested from the thousands, so is the compensation of our loving faith in the harvest infinitely fruitful.

It is then a wonderful and easy thing that we are doing. Plant one little simple seed of absolute Love. The soil of the Infinite is unceasingly receptive to our planting. It is productive, reproductive, and potent. A harvest is assured. It is a guarantee from the Universe to Itself. We all gain assurance from the wisdom we have always reaped as we have sown, and always will. As we rejoice in our present blessings, they are increased.

Think About What You're Thinking About

As Ernest Holmes was fond of saying, everyone thinks, but few people think about what they are thinking about. Spiritual Mind Treatment is thinking about what we are thinking about. Why? Whatever our thoughts rest upon consistently will continue to determine (and be) the course of our experience. There is no "take it or leave it" with the creativity of thought.

Love is the heart of the Spiritual Mind Treatment. By way of love, we can think clearly and intelligently. Knowing what we really are—a vigorous, poignant power of God in action—frees us into the wisdom of experience and the joy of loving self-leadership. This is the consciousness of prosperous being. This is letting go and letting clear thinking prevail.

Remember: when we see and know anything in a clear way, we can never again go back and accept a vague explanation of it. This is knowing what to do—when we need to know—and doing it: greeting everything in our world with love. The wisdom of love echoes down through the ages and says to each of us, "There is nothing but Mind, and there is nothing in your world but thought." Our inner world is invisible thought; in our outer world, thought becomes visible. If anyone ever interrupts you while you are in meditation and Spiritual Mind Treatment, asking, "What are you doing?" just say, "I am rearranging my outer world for the better."

Love heals the things we fear, and when we let go and let love do what it knows how to do, the doing becomes a great strength. When we learn to swim, fear of deep water vanishes, never to return. The thing we need to fix our minds *is* Mind.

If we are always against everything, when our good does come along, we might miss it or accidentally oppose it. As love unfolding, we focus on what we are *for*, discovering what is *right* about us and our world. Opportunities appear when we are prepared to meet them, greet them, and be responsible for them. Love appears when we let ourselves be love in action. Only people who take life for granted are bored with life. Each of us is a total idea in the Mind of God. What are we doing, and what are we going to do with and for *ourselves*?

Affirm: *I am a vigorous, poignant power of God in Action. As such, I am rearranging my outer world to fit my inner Positive Purpose.*

Chapter Fourteen

Live Life from Your Powerful Positive Purpose

By now, I trust you've realized that the work of those wishing to harness the Power of a Positive Purpose is the twofold action of affirmative prayer and spiritual realization. It is the power of the Spirit within, operating through Mind.

The metaphysician unifies with this Power and consciously directs it for constructive purposes. The result is the healing of the condition. The metaphysician constantly demonstrates the efficacy and magnitude of this Power opening the way for Infinite Spirit to reveal Itself within the mind, body, and experience of all who come to him or her for help. As it is stated in Isaiah 55:11, "So shall my word be that goeth forth out of my mouth . . . and it shall prosper in the thing whereto I send it."

It is the desire of metaphysicians to be of help to everyone who comes to them—including themselves. Their work includes contemplation and meditation, time for spiritual realization, and affirmative prayer. At that time, they embody a definite statement and acceptance of Truth. Thousands of people throughout the world who desire help for themselves and others are assisted every day by Spiritual Mind Treatment.

There is a pattern of perfection at the center of everything. There is a solution for every problem. The work of the metaphysical practitioner is to bring it forth through affirmative prayer and realization. It is the job of the practitioner constantly to be aware of this reality.

Consider these stories from people who embody the Truth that all the power, strength, peace, health, wealth, love, joy, clarity and knowledge of the Universe is theirs—is ours.

Know Your Mind, Body, and World Are Healthy

A healthy mind, body, and world are ours by right of consciousness. All we have to do is know it. For ourselves and for others.

Years ago, a call came in from a church member whose husband had suffered a stroke. There was damage to his tongue and voice box, and the doctors were very concerned about his condition.

The minister knew that the truth about this man had nothing to do with any verdict about him, and that the Power within him was free to unfold as his experience, unscathed by any concern around him. Outside the hospital room the doctor warned the minister, "He cannot speak. Do not stay too long, as it could stress him and hamper his recovery."

As the minister stepped into the room, he was greeted by the smiling eyes of the patient. The visit was brief, but important and powerful. Spiritual Mind Treatment was given and accepted, and as the minister was leaving, the man looked up at him and stated, "Thank you for coming; this means a lot to me."

Much to the doctor's amazement, the minister informed him that his patient could now speak. Today this man is in his second year of Science of Mind classes, enjoying his life, his family, and his golf game. He speaks perfectly.

Know Universal Power and Strength Are within You

Science of Mind teaches that we do not treat for *things*; we treat for the *consciousness* of the thing we wish to experience, and live from that state of consciousness. This is an example of originating a new cause in consciousness and allowing the law of Mind Its own outward, liberating action. Confidence in the Divine Self indwelling us puts in our hands all the power and strength of the Universe.

A woman looked at her life and the compensation she was receiving from the gift of her talents and asked, "Is that all there is?" Her answer came from within by way of the freedom she discovered through her study of Science of Mind.

She began to treat and accept the consciousness of prosperous being. She let go and let herself identify with a level of income above and beyond anything she had known before.

When the contract for her new position was agreed upon with her new employer, she looked at the whole event and affirmed for herself, "It is good enough to be true," and it was. She was being paid many thousands of dollars each month. Today, a year later, her skills are so appreciated that her income has again increased, and her husband has also received a promotion at work with an increase in pay.

Everything in her life is working out for the highest and best. She and her family are well, happy, prosperous, and very grateful for the blessings they have become to themselves and the world around them. As she stated to her fellow students in second-year Science of Mind class, "Does treatment work? You bet it does! And it's good enough to be true!"

> **Affirm:** *Everything in my life is working out for the highest and best. I, and my family, are well, happy, prosperous, and very grateful for the blessings we have become to ourselves and the world.*

Embrace Right Relationship with Yourself and Others

A side effect of these teachings is the discovery that a right relationship with yourself must by extension manifest as right relationship with others.

With tears in her eyes, a woman shared with her practitioner the story of her relationship with a man who would not make a commitment. This relationship had been going on for some time, but it did not seem to be going anywhere.

She asked her practitioner to treat that she marry this man. The practitioner refused the request, saying, "We will treat that *you* are the right person, and you are now free to demonstrate the right person as the right partner in your loving experience."

Eighteen months later, she spoke to her practitioner (who was also her minister) on the day of her wedding, saying, "I will never stop being thankful that we treated for the right relationship with myself and for the right person in my life." She had released the wrong relationship and affirmed the right one.

This had left her free to meet the right person in the right time and the right way. The couple declared, "I do!" and went on a beautiful honeymoon that has lasted for years and is getting better every day.

Focus Your Full Attention on the Indwelling Presence

With a heavy heart, a sad mother told her practitioner about her daughter's angry departure from home. She had not seen or heard from her daughter in over three years. The practitioner reminded her that the sincerity of the forgiveness we offer another is the measurement of the permanence, and extent, of the forgiveness we ourselves receive.

Two weeks of her knowing that "only perfect harmony of relationship prevails between my daughter and me" resulted in an early-morning phone call. She answered sleepily and heard the voice of the young woman on the line saying, "I love you, Mom. Can I come home?" The mother replied, "Oh, yes! Please, please come home!"

The daughter informed her mother she was now a grandmother. The daughter was bringing home a beautiful baby girl and was ready to start a new life for all of them.

Today, four years later, mother and grandmother are still celebrating. The baby is in kindergarten and is the light of her grandma's life. The daughter has completed her education, received her degree, and has a steady romantic relationship.

Her mother now says, "Words cannot express my appreciation of Science of Mind, my church, my ministers, and my practitioners. Through this wonderful study, I have found the joy of changing my mind and changing my life. My Spiritual Mind Treatment, four years ago, was one hundred percent effective. I am so grateful! My daughter returned and our lives are better than ever. I know my light is shining in such a wonderful way that others will want to know of this great Truth."

Now we are ready to live life from a powerful positive purpose. Now our thinking expands to include more of the Infinite Nature of God. Every day, remember the wisdom that echoes down through the ages: Ask and it shall be given you. Seek, and you shall find. Knock, and it shall be opened unto you.

God is a God of Love and of Joy. God—*in* all peoples, all races and all creeds—*is* all peoples, races, and creeds. We are each individualized beams of the Central Flame of God's Great Light. This living, loving believable God is the God we meet, and will forever meet, in every moment of eternity.

About the Author

A joyful and powerful teacher, Dr. Jay Scott Neale took a humor-filled approach to life, challenging people to wake up to their spiritual potential and take charge of their lives. He believed Science of Mind to be a teaching the world longs to embody. He committed his heart, mind, and energy to this great purpose.

Born in July 1940 and reared as a Baptist, he found himself in Southern California in the early 1960s, where he began his Science of Mind studies at Founders Church. Some of his early teachers included Dr. Fenwicke Holmes, Dr. Reginald Armour, Dr. Craig Carter, Dr. William Hornaday, Dr. George Bendal, and Dr. Edith Clark. He was a colleague and personal friend of Dr. Robert Bitzer and Dr. Raymond Charles Barker.

Jay received his first practitioner's license in 1968 and became a licensed minister in 1975, at the age of thirty-five. That same year, Jay and his wife Carol founded Tri-City

Church of Religious Science, which grew to 500 members. Jay received an honorary doctorate in 1983.

Jay was a steady contributor to *Creative Thought Magazine*, which featured his powerful Spiritual Mind Treatments, for three decades. He is the recipient of Religious Science International's Minister Meritorious and Minister of the Year awards and was awarded the Ernest Holmes Legacy Award.

Jay was an internationally recognized New Thought speaker and a joyful, powerful teacher. He was a member and/or board officer of many New Thought organizations, including The International New Thought Alliance (INTA), Religious Science International, Emerson Theological Institute, and the Affiliated New Thought Network (ANTN).

He challenged people to wake up to their spiritual potential and take charge of their lives, saying:

I believe we have a teaching the world is longing to embody.

My heart, mind, and energy are committed to this great purpose.

Printed in the USA
CPSIA information can be obtained
at www.ICGtesting.com
JSHW062025120424
61084JS00003B/64